The Recovery Journal: Partners Recovery Growth Index

By: Jason N. Hallman, MA, LPC, SRT

Reid Wood, MA, LPC, SRT

This book is dedicated to the millions of individuals before you who have decided to make recovery important in their lives. May you find the contents helpful as you too begin the road less travelled.

TABLE OF CONTENTS

INTRODUCTION..pg. 4

CHAPTER 1: Understanding Important Concepts in Addiction and Partner's Recovery Treatment...pg. 18-70

CHAPTER 2: Understanding the Role of Trauma within Addiction and Partner's Recovery..pg. 71-150

CHAPTER 3: The Importance of Boundaries in Healing from Trauma..pg. 151-199

CHAPTER 4: Navigating the Maze of Grief...................................pg. 200-277

CHAPTER 5: Understanding Physical and Relational Dynamics Within an Addictive System...pg. 278-312

CHAPTER 6: Developing a Vision and Moving Forward...................pg. 313-360

NOTES/REFERENCES..pg. 361-364

INTRODUCTION

Recovery for someone with acting-out/acting-in behavior is hard, but recovery for the partner of an addict can sometimes feel impossible. For the addict, recovery consists of stopping behaviors that he or she is aware of via boundaries, groups, and therapeutic processing. He or she learns to process their emotions and control their behavioral impulses. For the partner, recovery consists of overcoming the betrayal of the addict's secrecy regarding behavior he or she couldn't control and the traumatic impact this reality has on his or her emotional well-being and identity. It is the lack of control and the revelation that your partner is not the person he or she claimed to be that makes partner recovery difficult. Thus, it is YOU that must learn to trust again in someone who has proven to be untrustworthy in the past. This paradox can create a lot of anger and resentment. Let's be honest for a moment. You didn't choose to find yourself at this fork in the road of your relationship. When you made a commitment to your partner, you thought they would honor the expectations of being faithful, guarding and protecting your heart, emotionally connecting with you, and respecting your boundaries. If you are married, these expectations were likely articulated via your marital vows. Yet, a recent discovery or disclosure of acting out behavior by your partner has left you feeling betrayed, ashamed, abused, inadequate, angry, depressed, and anxious about your relationship. You feel stuck in an emotional whirlwind and find yourself staring at two possible directions to take at that proverbial fork in the road.

One path leads to divorce, heartbreak, familial separation, and the division of assets. This path also includes the loss of time and enmeshment in a romantic relationship that has often developed into a portion of your identity. In other words, to take that path, you realize that a part of you will cease to exist with the dissolution of the marriage. In the middle of the pain, this path can feel seductive as one wonders if the grass might be greener on the other side of divorce. However, an emotion-minded decision to divorce prematurely without taking time to process the pain of disclosure often ends in regret. Many pioneers in the recovery community encourage clients to avoid making major life decisions during the first year of recovery. This is due to the emotional and psychological volatility an individual experiences during the first year of the recovery process. We encourage partners to set healthy boundaries with their acting-out/acting-in partner and take time to process through the trauma of their betrayal to make wise-minded decisions about what is best for them in terms of relationship recovery.

Opposite of divorce, the second path towards reconciliation leads to the unknown anxiety associated with the question of "Can I trust him/her again?" That question typically leads to the second question of "Will things ever be the same?" The answers to those questions are as follows. Yes, trust is possible if your partner breaks through denial and works his or her recovery for the REST of his/her life and you are able to do the following: establish boundaries with him/her, work through the emotional and psychological trauma of betrayal, process your unresolved anger, grieve losses of his/her addiction, accept that your appearance/personality is not why he or she struggles with an addiction, and emotionally/psychologically get to a place of forgiveness/acceptance of past behavior. Sometimes, this process opens the doors of self-exploration, past trauma, and patterns of behavior that contributed to why you married your partner in the first place. It is through this individual introspection and therapeutic processing that both an addict and his or her partner must explore if true healing is possible in a relationship/marriage impacted by addiction. Once individual healing has taken place, it is then that one can begin to process the trust and non-related trust issues that led to difficulties in the relationship. As for the question pertaining to whether things will ever be the same again, there are two possibilities. The first possibility is that the disclosure of addiction leaves a painful wound in the relationship. Triggers will occasionally come and go but you each get to work on processing those difficult moments via healthy communication and conflict resolution. These types of couples both accept that things will never be the same while working to build a life that is focused on creating a new vision for the relationship despite the damage done by the addiction. The second possibility is the couple comes to view the disclosure as a catalyst to develop a healthier emotional, physical, spiritual relationship moving forward. Despite the pain and blame of how they came to their relational rock-bottom, this couple works to heal and move to a new future of connection via emotional, spiritual, physical intimacy. This probably sounds like a lot of work, but having anything in life worth fighting for typically requires a lot of effort.

You may be wondering how that can be possible with the level of anger, pain, and inadequacy you feel regarding the recent discovery of your partners acting-out/acting-in behavior. Let's start by dispelling the emotion-minded feelings you are experiencing with some reason-minded facts.

Fact 1: *He or She doesn't act out because you aren't good enough.*

Fact 2: *He or She acts out because they have an intimacy disorder and they cope with difficult emotions, distress, conflict, success/failure, and the lack of healthy attachment via acting-out/acting-in behaviors.*

Fact 3: *Addicts lie...especially when cornered in the shame of their addiction.* They didn't get here because of you despite all the gas lighting, controlling, or avoidant behaviors they may have projected towards you over the course of your relationship.

Fact 4: *He or She acts-out/acts-in because they are emotionally attached to their acting out behavior(s).*

Fact 5: *Your emotional pain matters and you are in a relationship with someone who likely hasn't learned how to empathize with your pain in healthy ways.*

Fact 6: *Despite owning that He or She has an addiction, your partner is still likely in denial regarding the gravity of His or Her addiction.* This is normal and is why extensive treatment is necessary to break through denial and establish healthy evidence-based treatment protocols.

Fact 7: *You deserve your own treatment to work through the pain you are experiencing.* Going to therapy doesn't mean that you are the problem. Some partners don't want to go to therapy because why should they have to talk about problems they didn't create? The reality is partners often experience PTSD-like criteria when learning that they have been lied to for a significant portion of their relationship.

Fact 8: *The trajectories of your recovery and the recovery of your partner will be different.* He or she can feel a lot better after dumping their secrets of acting-out/acting-in behavior. Now, you are left with the task of setting boundaries with them while you heal from the damage they caused. They get to work to earn your trust through their recovery behavior.

Fact 9: *Despite His or Her difficulty emotionally connecting with you, you still pursued the relationship and have maintained the relationship despite such deficits.* It is important to explore the patterns of behavior that brought two partners together and individual therapy is a good way to do that.

Fact 10: *Not loving His or Her partner is not a common reason that individuals act-out/act-in.* This is often a difficult concept for a partner to accept because on the surface it seems irrational to continually hurt the person you love with acting-out/acting-in behavior. The problem with addiction is irrational emotion-minded behavior. The following excerpt is from *The Recovery Journey: Sexual Recovery Growth Index*. Your partner who struggles with acting-out/acting-in behavior will be required to process this text as part of their recovery. It is important for partners to read *The Recovery Journal: Partners Recovery Growth Index* to understand the addiction cycle and what is required of the addict in working his or her recovery program.

The Big Book of Alcoholics Anonymous calls alcohol "cunning, baffling, and powerful." I think it is safe to say that these attributes can be assigned to any addictive behavior or substance. Let's start by considering the concept of cunning. Addiction is excellent at convincing you that your relationship with it really isn't that big of a deal. It tells you that real addicts are much worse than you and that the people in your life telling you that you have a problem are really the ones with the problem. If that doesn't work, addiction tells you that it will always be there for you and that you will not be able to manage life on your own. Cunning.

After a while, the consequences of the acting out/acting in behavior start to take shape. Maybe you notice your partner, wife, or children starting to distance themselves from you. Maybe you find yourself isolating from those closest to you at the expense of those connections. Inside, you tell yourself that you NEED to do better and attempt to set a boundary with the acting out/acting in behavior. This may last a few hours, days, weeks, sometimes months, but there is still something about the acting out/acting in experience that places it on your mind or shown via expressions of behavior. This frustrates you, but the frustration isn't enough to lead to sustained behavioral change. Baffling.

Weeks, months, and years seem to pass in a blur. The loneliness you feel inside is growing and you find yourself filling that void with acting out/acting in behavior despite the shame and frustration it is producing within you. You tell yourself, "I'm not going to do this again" or "This is the last time" only break your integrity in a repetitive cycle. Your anger bounces back and forth from yourself to your partner/wife/family/friends as they start setting boundaries telling you that they are going to have to move on in life without you. Yet, you still struggle with the thought/process of saying goodbye to your acting out/acting in behavior. Powerful.

Cunning. Baffling. Powerful. Three simplistic terms identified by Alcoholics Anonymous thanks to the visionaries Bill W. and Bob Smith, the founders of AA. If you are familiar with their story, you know it was through painstaking trial and error, acknowledging powerlessness, developing connections, developing introspection/insight, understanding the benefit of accountability, and many other factors that led to the development of the 12 steps.

Today, those 12 steps are being applied to all forms of acting out/acting in behavior and their usage has been a cornerstone in the recovery journey for millions of individuals.

You are probably asking, "Why is this relevant?" Therapeutic growth/progress occurs when individuals are willing to study themselves, ask the hard questions, face their fears...all while building connection/accountability with others going through similar struggles. Had Bill and Bob not taken the time to personally explore the who, what, when, and where of alcoholism, they likely wouldn't have cultivated a process built on developing insight into the why. Boundaries, accountability, spirituality, meetings, and recovery psychoeducation are all important in your recovery journey. However, understanding and processing the why of acting out/acting in behavior after developing boundaries, accountability, spirituality, attending meetings, and embracing recovery psychoeducation is often where significant healing can begin. The Recovery Journal: Sexual Recovery Growth Index is the bridge in that process, and it has been developed from countless hours of providing individual and group therapy to men, women, and their partners struggling with sexual addiction and intimacy anorexia.

As you can see, acting-out/acting-in behavior is pervasive in cunning, baffling, and powerful ways. Your partner cannot beat his or her addiction on their own and the reality is, your recovery from the damage of their behavior in your life likely requires some therapeutic help as well. My name is Jason Hallman, MA, LPC, SRT and my colleague is Reid Wood, MA, LPC, SRT. We are certified Sexual Recovery Therapists (SRT) through the American Association for Sex Addiction Therapy (AASAT) and take an integrated and holistic approach to treatment. Over the years, we have had the pleasure of watching countless individuals and families find healing from sexual acting out/acting in behaviors. Treating such circumstances is complex and requires trained clinicians who understand the individual intricacies of treatment. Feedback from clients who have completed other self-help studies, programs, etc. has taught us that one cannot take a one-size-fits-all approach to recovery. What works for one individual may not work for another. Thus, we focus on facilitating a recovery program that integrates material from multiple pioneers in the sexual recovery community with our own therapeutic model.

Like Bill and Bob with Alcoholics Anonymous, we are seeking to be visionaries in the treatment of sexual acting out/acting in issues that have become an epidemic in modern society. In a world where anyone can produce information about addiction via websites, books, recovery programs, podcasts, etc., it is just as easy to get lost in the tsunami of recovery knowledge (both good and bad) as it is to get lost in the emotional tsunami of your partner's acting out/acting in behavior. As a client, the last thing you want to be struggling with while working your emotional recovery from disclosure of your partner's acting-out/acting-in behavior is overstimulation from too much recovery material. Such an approach can possibly cause recovery burnout and discourage an individual from getting the most out of their recovery journey. This issue led us to develop a recovery tool in *The Recovery Journal: Partners Recovery Growth Index* to not only bridge the gap between a multitude of recovery theories, but also provide a client with therapeutic metric data, called the Partner Recovery Growth Index (PRGI), to enhance individual session treatment planning and track therapeutic progress.

We encourage you to learn/reflect on the terms, concepts, and Likert scales at the beginning of *The Recovery Journal: Partner Recovery Growth Index*. This conceptual knowledge will assist you in using *The Recovery Journal: Partner Recovery Growth Index* as a valuable recovery tool while exploring the psychological components of addiction and how they have played a role in the relationship you have with your partner. Remember, recovery is not a list of tasks to be completed as fast as possible. Healthy recovery work takes time, and we encourage you to take your time when reflecting on your weekly entries in *The Recovery Journal: Partner Recovery Growth Index*.

Also, please note that the PRGI will only provide insight if you are being 100% honest with yourself. It is imperative that you do not score yourself out of fear of disappointing others or your therapist. Being honest with yourself and others is an integral part of healing, and this concept will make more and more sense as we continue our work together. We look forward to facilitating the next phase of your therapeutic growth and feel privileged to be a part of your recovery. May our journey together over the next year be filled with therapeutic insight and growth as you learn to love and trust yourself and hopefully your partner again.

Jason N. Hallman, MA, LPC, SRT

Reid Wood, MA, LPC, SRT

Chapter 1: Understanding Important Concepts in Addiction and Partner's Recovery Treatment

If you are new to the world of recovery, you are probably feeling overwhelmed by the information and jargon associated with addiction therapy. This section of the text offers some definitions of recovery terms, treatment methodologies, and treatment tools associated with our recovery program. Take a moment to read through the terms and familiarize yourself with the material. Be sure to highlight anything in the text you have questions about, and your therapist or life coach can clarify your concerns during your next individual appointment.

Recovery Terms:

Accountability Partner – An individual that a person in recovery calls to check-in triggers, process emotions, and assist in holding an individual accountable for recovery goals. Ideally, accountability partners are members of a clinician-led work group and/or a 12-step support group for the issue that the individual is addressing via therapy.

Acting-In – A behavioral addiction to internalizing one's emotions and controlling, avoiding/withholding emotional and/or physical intimacy from others. Intimacy Anorexia is an extreme form of acting-in behavior.

Acting-Out – A behavioral addiction to substances, process behaviors (i.e. sex, work, food, gambling, exercise, etc.), compulsive attachment (co-dependency, high-risk relationships, etc.), and feelings (i.e. fear, self-loathing, risk, etc.).

Boundary – A individually specific behavioral barrier that is internally and externally motivated to prevent harm and possibly restore trust. This barrier is only a boundary when it has a behavioral consequence associated with breaking the boundary.

Clinician-led Work Group – A therapeutic group that is led by one or more clinicians with the purpose of processing therapeutic exercises to cope with addiction, trauma, and emotional regulation issues.

Codependency – A type of compulsive attachment behavioral addiction that is predicated on rescuing behaviors, poor boundaries, and identity issues associated with the need to help others to distract from dealing with one's own individual issues.

Consequence – A behavioral response that is implemented when a behavioral boundary has been broken. (i.e. a sex addict must have monitoring software on his phone after breaking the boundary of looking at pornography).

Full Disclosure – A therapeutically-led event where a sex addict discloses all the sexual acting-out behaviors that have occurred throughout the course of his or her life and/or his or her current relationship.

Mindfulness – The process of being emotionally and physically present in the here and now. A person practicing mindfulness is aware of what is going on in the mind and body and feels connected to his or her present reality.

Parts-work – The process of psychologically and mindfully attuning to a "part" of the self and connecting/communicating to that part in a validating and/or nurturing response.

Self-care – The process of doing a behavior that is physically, emotionally, or spiritually beneficial.

Self-persecution – The process of devaluing, criticizing, and shaming oneself for experiencing anxiety, behaviors, mistakes, unwanted traits, and unwanted outcomes.

Self-talk – The internal and external dialogue an individual has with himself or herself.

Self-worth – An individual's perception of themselves and the value he or she brings to life.

Sponsor – An individual affiliated with a 12-step program who is a mentor for people new to working a 12-step program.

Typically, a sponsor has completed the 12-steps and is currently in sobriety. Getting a sponsor is an important part of the recovery process.

Spontaneous Separation – The process of separating from one's partner without formally developing a therapeutic plan for the separation.

Staggered Disclosure – The process of spontaneously confessing acting-out behavior to a partner outside of a therapeutic setting over the course of days, weeks, months, or years. This form of disclosure is re-traumatizing to a partner and often delays therapeutic progress.

Support group – A non-clinician-led group that is topic/issue based. 12-step programs are considered support groups.

Therapeutic Separation – The process of separating from one's partner with therapeutic goals and objectives under the treatment of a therapist. Therapeutic separation is sometimes necessary for emotional healing in relationships impacted by sexual addiction.

Types of Treatment:

Behavioral Treatment – a therapeutic model that focuses on positive/negative reinforcement of wanted/unwanted behaviors.

> Example: Installing monitoring software on a phone to reduce/discourage the viewing of sexual content and establishing the punishment/consequence of having to sleep on the couch for a week if one was to look at sexual material would be an example of behavioral treatment.

Cognitive Treatment – a therapeutic model that focuses on challenging/changing one's negative self-talk that impacts one's emotional state and perspective on reality.

> Example: Instead of telling oneself, "I'm not good enough for my partner", one could say, "I'm enough and I get to set boundaries with my partner while I heal from the feelings of inadequacy generated by his or her acting out behavior."

Dialectical-Behavioral Treatment – a therapeutic model that focuses on challenging dialectical thinking (all or nothing) via the balance of one's emotion-mind and reason-mind into a wise-mind state via various skills and emotional regulation techniques.

> Example: Learning to recognize that it is okay to acknowledge feelings/emotions, however, it is how we respond to them within ourselves and with others that makes all the difference.

Experiential Treatment – a therapeutic model that focuses on exposing a client to unwanted circumstances, feelings, experiences, to desensitize an individual to certain stimuli and assist in rewiring neuropathways in the brain to healthily process past trauma.

> Example: Talking to group members about your feelings is an experiential treatment for someone who has intimacy anorexia or other fears related to emotional vulnerability.

Psychodrama Treatment – a therapeutic model that focuses on processing conflict/issues via empty chair exercises, role-playing, etc. in front of a therapeutic group.

> Example: Role-playing how to communicate feelings/set boundaries with your partner due to his or her acting out

behavior is an example of psychodrama. Another example would be having an external dialogue with your partner's addiction or addiction(s) via the use of multiple chairs in which you role-play/personify each addiction.

Psychoeducational Treatment – a therapeutic model that focuses on teaching concepts, theories, and strategies for addressing therapeutic issues.

Example: Learning about addiction terminology, the addiction cycle, setting boundaries, coping strategies, etc.

Transactional Analysis Treatment (TA) – a therapeutic model that focuses on the internal family system (Schwartz, 1995) relationship between the inner parent, inner adult, and inner child. This model explores how the parent-adult-child (PAC) interacts with other parent-adult-child (PAC) dynamics within the self and in external relationships. These interactions are called transactions that are therapeutically analyzed. Our program uses concepts of Internal Family Systems (IFS), TA and the PAC to teach clients how to develop healthy attachment.

Parent
Adult
Child

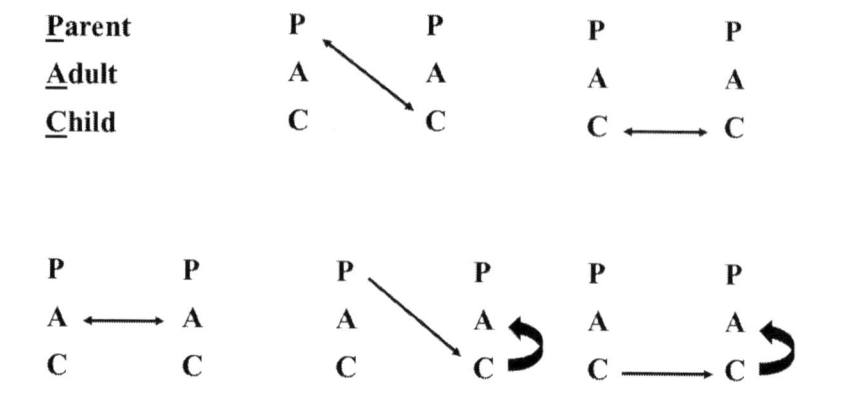

```
P       P ↖      P       P          P       P
A        A  ↘   A        A          A       A
C        C       C        C          C ←——→ C
```

```
P       P        P ↖     P          P       P
A ←——→ A         A    ↘  A ↶        A       A ↶
C       C        C       C          C ——→  C
```

Example: An individual who struggles with acting out/acting in behavior often struggles with an unnurtured/traumatized inner-child who sometimes responds to emotions in avoidant/self-persecutory/explosive ways. TA is used to analyze parent-to-child and child-to-child dynamics that teach an individual to re-parent their inner-child in healthy/nurturing ways. This allows an individual to mature emotionally via therapeutic interventions.

Treatment Model:

Most quality treatment programs for sexual acting-out and acting-in issues have a multi-faceted approach that is rooted in building second-order change behaviors into a family system. To achieve this, our program features individual therapy and clinician-led groups for the addict and partner, with the expectation that the addict attends a 12-step program in addition to a clinician-led work group. Once both the addict and spouse have stabilized his or her individual recovery, clients can speak with their therapist regarding the progression to couple's therapy. According to Dr. Patrick Carnes, recovery can take 3-5 years of work. It is not something that can be expedited and requires time to build new neuropathways of recovery and healthy coping behaviors that are in opposition to the addiction neuropathways that have likely been present for most of your partner's life. If your partner is not participating in individual therapy, a clinician-led work group, and a 12-step program, the 3–5-year timetable will likely need to be expanded and the efficacy of treatment will be reduced. On the other side of the spectrum, your recovery is equally important to the efficacy of treatment. Failing to address the trauma of disclosure, past experiences, and boundary issues will likely increase the timetable of the recovery process. One of the frustrations of doing addiction work is seeing an addict make significant strides from a therapeutic perspective only to see marital conflict remain due to a partner's unwillingness to get help to address the trauma he or she deals with every day. One of the sources of continued trauma is the lack of completing a full disclosure during the first 6 months of the recovery process.

Full Disclosure:

Full disclosure is an important component to marital recovery after the discovery of sexual acting-out behavior. At this point, you may have already had your partner tell you everything regarding his or her acting out behavior. However, sometimes information is forgotten, compartmentalized, omitted, or withheld when staggered disclosure has occurred outside of a therapeutic setting. Full disclosure is an opportunity for you to hear everything your partner has done from a sexual acting out perspective in the office of a clinician. Prior to full disclosure, your partner will work with his or her therapist to reflect and identify all behaviors that are to be disclosed and remove any details from the disclosure that would be harmful to you (i.e. body characteristics, ethnicity, sexual positions, etc.). However, if anything has occurred that is relevant (i.e. sleeping with someone in your bed, sleeping with/sexting your friend/family member, same-sex behavior, etc.) this behavior will be disclosed to allow you to set appropriate boundaries with such individuals, locations, or items. After your partner reads his or her disclosure, you have an opportunity to ask questions that are not hurtful to you. After the questions period, you will be able to process your emotions with your therapist one on one. This experience, despite the pain and anxiety associated with it, will allow you to grieve the losses associated with your partner's betrayal and work towards restoring trust in the relationship. While full disclosure is not required to work the program, it is a healthy component available to assist clients in the recovery process.

Dr. Douglas Weiss <u>5 Commandments of Recovery</u>

1. Prayer
2. Calls to Accountability Partners
3. Reading Recovery Material
4. Attending Meetings/Counseling
5. Prayer

Every sports enthusiast knows that fundamentals are key to high-level athletic performance. Without fundamentals, the best game-plans are in-effective on the field or court of play. The 5 Commandments of Recovery are the daily/weekly fundamentals to a healthy behavioral, spiritual, experiential, and psychoeducational recovery plan for acting-out/acting-in behavior(s). It is our expectation that your partner is making the 5 commandments of recovery a daily component to his or her life. While attending meetings/counseling is not a daily requirement, there isn't an excuse for not consistently doing the other commandment items each day.

Dr. Douglas Weiss <u>Intimacy Anorexia (IA) Dailies</u>

1. Lead your partner in prayer.
2. Share 2 affirmations regarding your partner to him/her.
3. Share 2 feelings with context that do not involve criticism of your partner.
4. Initiate some form of an intimate activity with your partner (this does not have to be sexual and can be a walk together, candlelight dinner, etc.).

The IA dailies is an experiential treatment technique to reduce anxiety associated with developing emotional intimacy. If you or your partner struggle with Intimacy Anorexia, the IA dailies are an important exercise to incorporate into your relationship every day.

Reflect on your daily routine and the routine of your significant other. What are some strategies you can take to implement the IA dailies into your relationship if IA is present in you or your partner?

_____

_____

_____

Partner Recovery Growth Index (Hallman and Wood, 2023)

The Partner Recovery Growth Index (PRGI) is a therapeutic tool that is used to measure one's therapeutic progress in recovery. It also can be used to develop insight into one's recovery struggles and assist in informing individual therapeutic interventions. It is important that you understand the definitions of each metric in the index so that you can properly score yourself each week. The PRGI will also serve as your group syllabus to reference reading and exercise requirements to be completed before each group.

To establish a baseline, read through the definitions of each metric and circle where you feel you currently are on the Likert scale. Explain your rationale for your ranking in the space provided.

DENIAL – A psychological and behavioral process of avoidance in which an individual is confronted with an issue and/or reality and chooses to reject and and/or deny evidence or facts supporting the issue/reality. In the process of addiction, denial is used to protect an individual from feeling the emotional pain associated with his or her partner's acting-out/acting-in behavior.

DENIAL 1 2 3 4 5 6 7 8 9 10

1 = Believing my partner isn't an addict, denying my partner's progress, and/or denying the hurt and pain I am feeling because of my partner's addiction.

10 = Consistently feeling/expressing the pain caused by my partner's behavior and adjusting boundaries when appropriate due to therapeutic insight and progress.

Rationale:_____

_____

_____

ANXIETY-MANAGEMENT – The use of therapeutic processing tools to manage anxiety in a healthy way. Note that this metric is not concerned with the amount of anxiety you feel as some individuals are genetically and environmentally predisposed to experience a higher level of anxiety than others on a regular basis. The purpose of anxiety management is not to numb/avoid/minimize anxiety, but to acknowledge and process anxiety in healthy ways. Examples would include: *(Journaling with a feelings wheel to identify emotions behind one's anxiety. Talking with others/processing emotions behind one's anxiety. Practicing mindfulness and/or deep breathing. Using cognitive strategies to reduce catastrophizing thoughts. Channeling your anxiety into various types of exercise or yard work. Etc.)*

ANXIETY MANAGEMENT   1   2   3   4   5   6   7   8   9   10

1 = Avoiding anxiety triggers and anxious feelings/sensations in my body
10 = Acknowledging anxiety and using it to provide insight into what is important

Rationale:

ANGER MANAGEMENT – The use of therapeutic processing tools to manage/express anger in a healthy way. The purpose of anger management is not to numb/avoid/minimize anger, but to acknowledge and process anger in healthy ways. Examples would include: *(Journaling with a feelings wheel to identify emotions behind one's anger. Talking with others/processing emotions behind one's anger. Writing anger letters to process with a therapist. Yelling into a pillow. Channeling anger via various types of exercise or yard work. Etc.)*

ANGER MANAGEMENT   1 2 3 4 5 6 7 8 9 10

1 = Having explosive outbursts, making threats, yelling, stuffing, devaluing, withholding, and other child-like dynamics when experiencing anger

10 = Consistently expressing anger in an adult-to-adult dynamic and externally processing anger via the use of therapeutic tools

Rationale: _____

_____

_____

DEPRESSION MANAGEMENT – The use of therapeutic processing tools to manage/process depression in a healthy way. Learning to live outside the victim orientation and being proactive as opposed to reactive. Taking behavioral baby-steps towards one's mission statement in life and relationships. Examples would include: *(Journaling with a feelings wheel to identify emotions behind one's depression. Talking with others/processing emotions behind one's depression. Writing anger letters to externalize anger instead of turning anger inward to decrease depression symptoms. Developing and working healthy sleep, exercise, and nutrition plans as a form of self-care. Challenging negative self-talk and self-persecution.*

DEPRESSION MANAGEMENT   1 2 3 4 5 6 7 8 9 10

1 = Choosing to engage in the victim orientation via avoiding emotional processing, not practicing self-care, and self-loathing every day for the past 7+ days
10 = Consistently choosing to use therapeutic tools, practice self-care, and take behavioral baby steps towards one's mission statement in life every day for the past 14 days

Rationale:_____

_____

_____

SHAME MANAGEMENT – Feeling that you are a bad person or a mistake. This is sometimes the product of trauma and regretful experience (s). Shame is distinct from guilt in that it is tied to an individual's identity. Guilt is not tied to identity and is related to behavior.

Shame *= I'm a bad partner/person for having a partner who looks at pornography.*

Guilt *= I feel bad for hurting my partner's feelings when yelling at them, but I get to apologize. (i.e. I'm a good person who made some mistakes and I get to receive his or her grace and work on my recovery.).*

SHAME MANAGEMENT | 1 2 3 4 5 6 7 8 9 10

1 = Believing I'm a bad person or a mistake (i.e. I'm a bad wife/I'm unlovable)
10 = Believing I'm a good person who made some mistakes

Rationale:_____

_____

_____

CO-DEPENDENCY – A compulsive attachment addiction that is rooted in rescuing behavior, poor boundaries, and a compulsive desire to "fix" others. A function of co-dependency is often to help others to distract oneself from his or her own issues. When there is nothing to fix or advice is rejected, co-dependents often struggle with self-worth issues. Therapeutic progress in treatment of co-dependent issues is learning to set healthy boundaries, identify/process one's own emotions, and developing a healthy mission statement for one's life that transitions away from an external locus of control to an internal locus of control.

CO-DEPENDENCY 1 2 3 4 5 6 7 8 9 10

1 = Exhibiting rescuing behavior, failure to set boundaries, failure to implement consequences for boundary failures, and failing to process one's own issues during the past 7+ days.
10 = I have set/executed boundaries, taken behavioral baby steps towards my individual mission statement, acknowledged/processed my emotions, and living a life that is more internally than externally motivated

Rationale:_____

_____

_____

BOUNDARIES – Setting, maintaining, and implementing specific boundaries/consequences with yourself and others. Maintaining boundary consequences despite fear, anxiety, or loneliness. Not using vague boundaries to justify withholding despite significant sobriety in the life of your partner.

BOUNDARIES 1 2 3 4 5 6 7 8 9 10

1 = A total lack of boundaries or the use of vague boundaries to justify withholding.

10 = Consistently maintaining boundaries and implementing consequences when boundaries are violated.

Rationale:_____

_____

_____

TRUST – Exhibiting trust in your partner concerning his or her recovery work and allowing boundaries/consequences to work for you (i.e. Not needing to scroll through your partners phone or stare at his or her eyes when being out in public settings). Exhibiting trust in yourself to make good decisions in wise mind.

TRUST	1 2 3 4 5 6 7 8 9 10

1 = Obsessing about your partner's recovery (OCD/co-dependency/anxiety), ignoring your partner's recovery work (denial/avoidance) and/or doubting your ability to make good decisions in the past 7+ days

10 = Consistently allowing your boundaries/consequences to work for you, expressing emotions in healthy transparent ways during FANOS check-ins and working towards building healthy attachment.

Rationale:_____

_____

_____

ACTING-IN – Intentionally withholding love and intimacy from my partner (when not related to a timed boundary consequence) in response to anger or fear of being emotionally hurt again.

ACTING-IN	1 2 3 4 5 6 7 8 9 10

1 = I withheld emotional/spiritual/physical intimacy in the past 7 days

10 = 6+ months of continuous emotional/spiritual/physical engagement

Rationale:_____

_____

_____

FORGIVENESS – Emotionally and psychologically working through the grief process associated with your betrayal and getting to a place where you decide to no longer hold the betrayal against the individual who hurt you (*This does not mean you forget what happened, but it means that you are choosing to let it go and allow boundaries/consequences to be the protective barrier in your life/relationship moving forward*). Forgiveness is ultimately for you and not the individual who betrayed you. However, forgiveness is critical in a relationship if one desires reconciliation and critical for emotionally and psychologically moving on after a relationship is over.

FORGIVENESS   1 2 3 4 5 6 7 8 9 10

1 = Holding onto anger/resentment/bitterness and refusing to consider forgiveness

10 = I have fully processed my grief, accepted the betrayal, set boundaries, and reached a level of peace due to forgiveness

Rationale:_____

_____

_____

CONFLICT RESOLUTION – The ability to use healthy assertiveness/active listening, empathy, and adult-to-adult communication skills to resolve conflict. The purpose of healthy conflict resolution is not to avoid/minimize conflict, but to use conflict to grow one's relationships.

CONFLICT RESOLUTION	1 2 3 4 5 6 7 8 9 10

1 = Displaying parent-to-child or child-to-child dynamics during conflict or avoiding conflict via people pleasing behaviors

10 = Consistently using healthy assertiveness and active listening with empathy to resolve conflict or reach a compromise in life every day for the past 14 days

Rationale:_____

_____

_____

SELF-WORTH – The value an individual sees in himself or herself in his or her respective environment. For example, most people find themselves with decreased self-worth when learning about infidelity as the experience generates the emotion-minded belief of "What's wrong with me?"

SELF-WORTH 1 2 3 4 5 6 7 8 9 10

1 = Feeling/believing I'm inadequate every day in the past 7+ days

10 = Feeling/believing I'm an adequate individual whose worth is not tied to another individual's behavior each day for the past 3+ months

Rationale:_____

_____

_____

SELF CARE – The ability to understand one's needs/limitations and taking behavioral and psychological steps to promote one's well-being in times of stress. Examples of self-care would be the following: *(Practicing mindfulness, treating yourself to a nice meal, going for a walk, setting boundaries at work, setting boundaries in a relationship, setting boundaries with friends/family, working one's recovery, reading a book, praying, building something for fun, taking a vacation, etc.).*

SELF-CARE   1 2 3 4 5 6 7 8 9 10

1 = Neglecting self-care behaviors/No self-care behaviors during the past 7+ days
10 = Consistently practicing self-care behaviors each day for the past year

Rationale:_____
_____
_____

How to use *The Recovery Journal: Partners Recovery Growth Index* to get the most out of group and individual treatment

Now that you are familiar with the theoretical concepts we will reference during group and the metrics associated with the PRGI, let's talk about how to use *The Recovery Journal*. Each week of group will be represented by 2 pages in *The Recovery Journal* that list the following headings: Week , Date , Exercises to Complete , Objectives , Notes - Insights - Things to Explore in Therapy , Accountability Issues – Goals for the Week , Partner Recovery Growth Index . Each heading is important to reference each week of group as this book will become your syllabus, group therapy journal, and weekly PRGI self-assessment.

Weekly Steps for The Recovery Journal

1. Each week, you will reference *The Recovery Journal* and process exercises from the book for that specific week.

2. Pay attention to the **Objectives** for the week and feel free to take notes in the **Notes - Insights - Things to Explore in Therapy** section of the journal during any psychoeducational portion of the group or while reflecting on insights after group.

3. At times during workbook exercise processing, when you or others are sharing, you might develop important insights into yourself regarding your recovery. This is another time to use the **Notes - Insights - Things to Explore in Therapy** section to reference when meeting with your individual clinician during your next individual session. You may also identify accountability issues or goals you would like to develop related to group material. You can list such items in the **Accountability Issues – Goals for the Week** section.

4. At the close of each group, reflect on the past week of your life and complete the **Partner Recovery Growth Index** section.

5. If you have an individual session before the next group meeting, take *The Recovery Journal* with you to the session to process any relevant insights.

6. Repeat the process starting with step 1 the following week.

We hope you find *The Recovery Journal: Partners Recovery Growth Index* a useful tool in your recovery. We look forward to facilitating this process with you during the next 22 weeks of your therapeutic journey!

Week 2

DATE	EXERCISES TO COMPLETE
	Read pages 49-60 and complete exercises: 1-1 and 1-2

OBJECTIVES

- Exploring the role of emotions in recovery.
- Applying the DBT technique of wise mind to process emotions.

NOTES – INSIGHTS – THINGS TO EXPLORE IN THERAPY

_____
_____
_____
_____
_____
_____
_____
_____
_____

ACCOUNTABILITY ISSUES – GOALS FOR THE WEEK

_____
_____
_____
_____
_____
_____
_____
_____
_____
_____

PARTNER RECOVERY GROWTH INDEX (PRGI)

DENIAL 1 2 3 4 5 6 7 8 9 10

1 = Believing my partner isn't an addict, denying my partner's progress, and/or denying the hurt and pain I am feeling because of my partner's addiction.

10 = Consistently feeling/expressing the pain caused by my partner's behavior and adjusting boundaries when appropriate due to therapeutic insight and progress.

ANXIETY MANAGEMENT 1 2 3 4 5 6 7 8 9 10

1 = Avoiding anxiety triggers and anxious feelings/sensations in my body

10 = Acknowledging anxiety and using it to provide insight into what is important

ANGER MANAGEMENT 1 2 3 4 5 6 7 8 9 10

1 = Having explosive outbursts, making threats, yelling, stuffing, devaluing, withholding, and other child-like dynamics when experiencing anger

10 = Consistently expressing anger in an adult-to-adult dynamic and externally processing anger via the use of therapeutic tools

DEPRESSION MANAGEMENT 1 2 3 4 5 6 7 8 9 10

1 = Choosing to engage in the victim orientation via avoiding emotional processing, not practicing self-care, and self-loathing every day for the past 7+ days

10 = Consistently choosing to use therapeutic tools, practice self-care, and take behavioral baby steps towards one's mission statement in life every day for the past 14 days

SHAME MANAGEMENT 1 2 3 4 5 6 7 8 9 10

1 = Believing I'm a bad person or a mistake (i.e. I'm a bad wife/I'm unlovable)

10 = Believing I'm a good person who made some mistakes

CO-DEPENDENCY 1 2 3 4 5 6 7 8 9 10

1 = Exhibiting rescuing behavior, failure to set boundaries, failure to implement consequences for boundary failures, and failing to process one's own issues during the past 7+ days.

10 = I have set/executed boundaries, taken behavioral baby steps towards my individual mission statement, acknowledged/processed my emotions, and living a life that is more internally than externally motivated

BOUNDARIES 1 2 3 4 5 6 7 8 9 10

1 = A total lack of boundaries or the use of vague boundaries to justify withholding.

10 = Consistently maintaining boundaries and implementing consequences when boundaries are violated.

TRUST 1 2 3 4 5 6 7 8 9 10

1 = Obsessing about your partner's recovery (OCD/co-dependency/anxiety), ignoring your partner's recovery work (denial/avoidance) and/or doubting your ability to make good decisions in the past 7+ days

10 = Consistently allowing your boundaries/consequences to work for you, expressing emotions in healthy transparent ways during FANOS check-ins and working towards building healthy attachment.

ACTING-IN 1 2 3 4 5 6 7 8 9 10

1 = I withheld emotional/spiritual/physical intimacy in the past 7 days

10 = 6+ months of continuous emotional/spiritual/physical engagement

FORGIVENESS 1 2 3 4 5 6 7 8 9 10

1 = Holding onto anger/resentment/bitterness and refusing to consider forgiveness

10 = I have fully processed my grief, accepted the betrayal, set boundaries, and reached a level of peace due to forgiveness

CONFLICT RESOLUTION 1 2 3 4 5 6 7 8 9 10

1 = Displaying parent-to-child or child-to-child dynamics during conflict or avoiding conflict via people pleasing behaviors

10 = Consistently using healthy assertiveness and active listening with empathy to resolve conflict or reach a compromise in life every day for the past 14 days

SELF-WORTH 1 2 3 4 5 6 7 8 9 10

1 = Feeling/believing I'm inadequate every day in the past 7+ days

10 = Feeling/believing I'm an adequate individual whose worth is not tied to another individual's behavior each day for the past 3+ months

SELF-CARE 1 2 3 4 5 6 7 8 9 10

1 = Neglecting self-care behaviors/No self-care behaviors during the past 7+ days

10 = Consistently practicing self-care behaviors each day for the past year

Wheel of Emotions

Identifying emotions can be a real struggle for a sex addict and sometimes his or her partner. This comes from years of escaping uncomfortable emotions through an addict's acting-out/acting-in behavior and/or the partner escaping uncomfortable emotions via rescuing behaviors towards the addict or others. The more an addict acts-out or withholds via acting-in, the more the inner-child can gain control of what emotions are felt and expressed. Part of the therapy process is learning how to identify and express emotions in a healthy manner. There are two types of emotions: primary emotions and secondary emotions. Primary emotions are automatic emotional responses to a situation with common facial expressions that are recognized across cultural lines. Examples of primary emotions are fear, sadness, shame, joy, peace, anger, guilt, and feeling valued, etc. Secondary emotions are feelings that are in response to a primary emotion. An example of a secondary emotion would be fear of walking up on a snake and then experiencing anxiety over the situation. In addition to these emotions, our work in treating sexual addiction has led to the identification of primary emotions that most individuals in the sexual acting-out/acting-in cycle experience which are shame, despair, anxiety, inadequacy, anger, and self-loathing. To assist in the process exploring emotions, we have created an emotion wheel to help the client identify their emotions. *We encourage you to refer to this wheel when **journaling, checking-in**, completing the **IA dailies** communication exercise, and the **FANOS** communication exercise with your partner.*

Wheel of Emotions

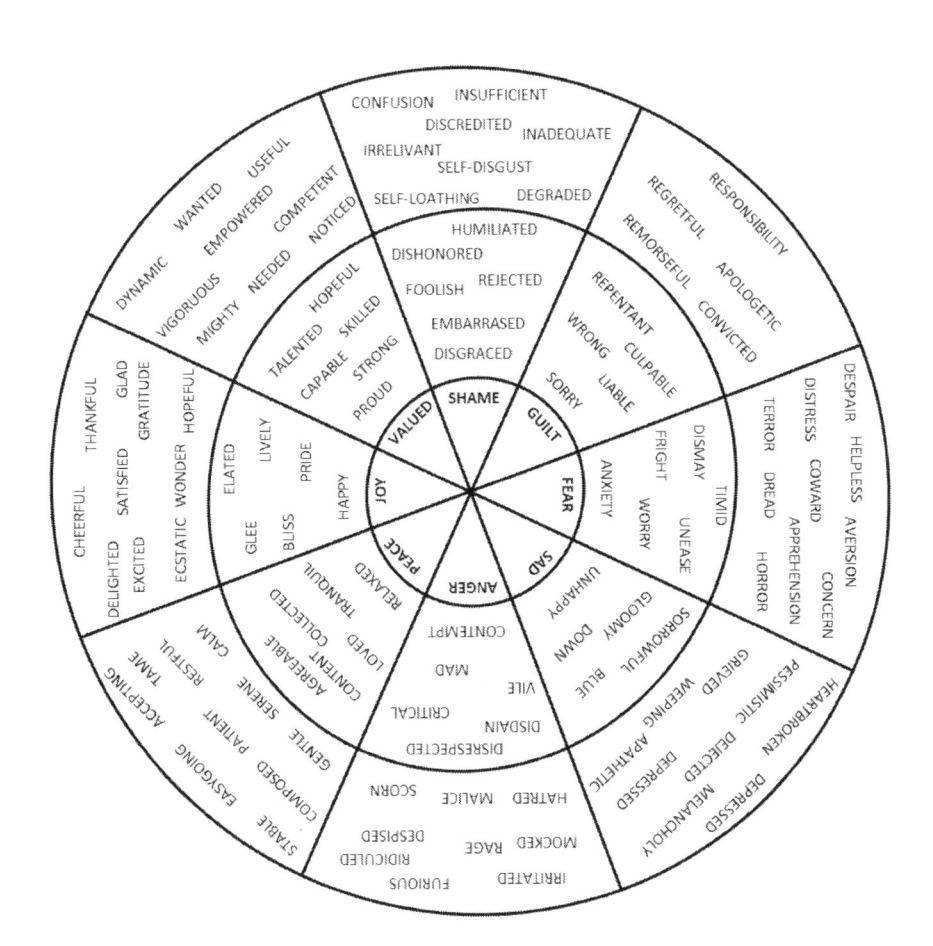

EXERCISE 1-1: REFLECTION ON EMOTIONS

When reflecting on the wheel of emotions, which emotions are the most difficult for you to communicate to others?

_____

_____

_____

In what ways do you think emotional vulnerability is important in intimate relationships?

_____

_____

_____

In what ways do you think emotional vulnerability is important in your recovery?

_____

_____

_____

Marsha Linehan - WISE MIND MODEL

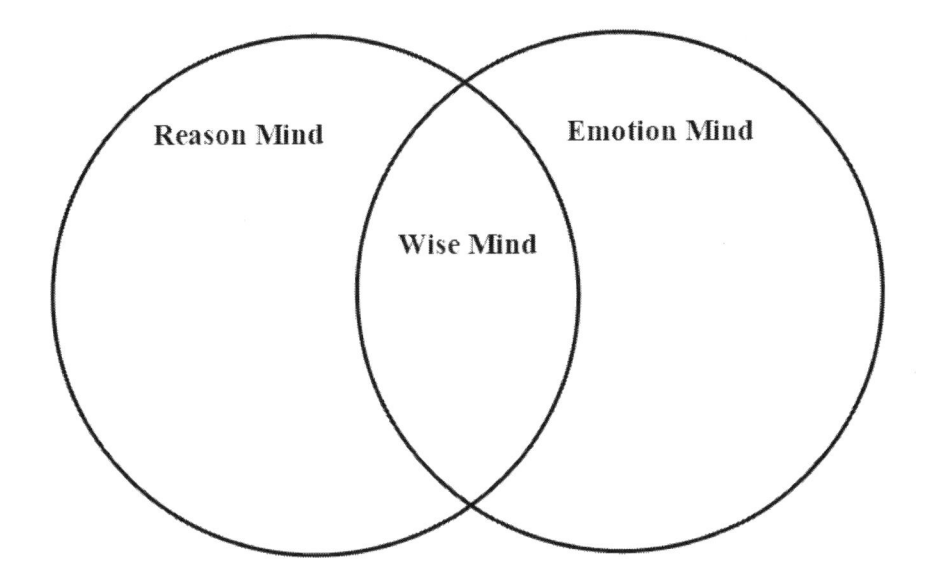

Venn diagram with two overlapping circles labeled "Reason Mind" and "Emotion Mind", with the overlap labeled "Wise Mind".

When a sex addict is acting-out/acting-in, the emotional state of being is in charge. The Wise Mind Model is a helpful dialectical tool to prevent making an emotional decision. This Venn diagram shows how an individual makes decisions based off the emotion mind, reason mind, or wise mind. When in the emotion mind, the emotions are in control and an individual makes impulsive choices with little concern for the consequences to self or others. When in the reason mind, all decisions are made using facts and logic. This state of mind has no regard for emotions. In the case of addiction, an addicts' reason mind often views negative emotions as problems to be solved, avoided, or numbed. While this sounds good in theory, it can lead to poor choices being made due to the discounting of the emotional self. Ideally, wise mind is where the best decisions are made because all states of mind are given a voice. Wise mind is a balance between the emotion mind and reason mind. It pays respect to both ways of thought and allows for a more balanced decision to be made. Understanding and applying the wise mind model is imperative to recovery because 100% of acting-out/acting-in occurs when an individual is in emotion mind. We know this because if individuals were accessing their reason mind, they would acknowledge the consequences of acting-out/acting-in and cope with their pain agents/emotions via healthy recovery behaviors.

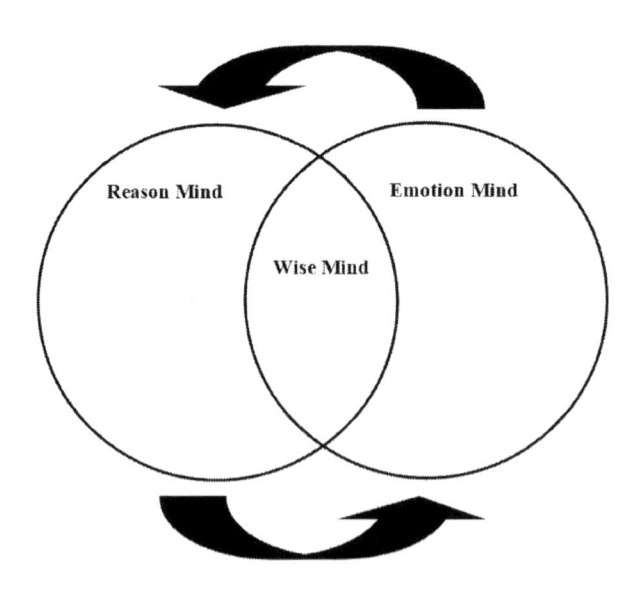

Example: Let's say an individual is struggling with the emotion-minded belief of "I'm a bad person." A person using the wise mind model would use his reason mind to ask, "Okay. I know I am feeling like a bad person, but what are the factual good and unhealthy behaviors I have exhibited in my life and how have others factually responded to me." When taking this reason minded inventory, one can challenge the emotion mind to find the balance. In our example, one might find the wise mind belief to be, "I'm feeling guilty for my acting out behavior, but I know I'm a good person who has made some mistakes, and I get to continue working my recovery." This wise minded belief factors in the true emotions behind the emotion minded belief while acknowledging all facts (good/bad via a logical unbiased lens) surrounding the individual's experience. Take a moment to apply some of these concepts in the exercise on the next page.

EXERCISE 1-2: WISE MIND APPLICATION

Reflect on times when you have been triggered by your partner's acting out/acting in behavior. Were you in emotion mind, wise mind, or reason mind when making that choice? Explain.

_____

_____

_____

_____

_____

How has your emotion-mindedness or reason-mindedness impacted your ability to be emotionally present during difficult circumstances? What was/is the cost of those responses in your life?

_____

_____

_____

_____

_____

Now let's apply the wise mind model to a current emotion-minded trigger. Think back to an experience that led to you having an emotion-minded thought/belief (example: you catch your partner looking at pornography and thought "I'm not enough"). Write your thought/belief in the emotion-mind circle. Then, list all the facts (positive and negative) associated with your life surrounding the experience in the reason mind circle. If you notice true emotions surfacing when looking at those facts, write them inside the emotion mind circle. Now reflect on both circles and ask yourself, "What is the balance between these two circles?" Write the balanced wise mind statement in the wise mind circle.

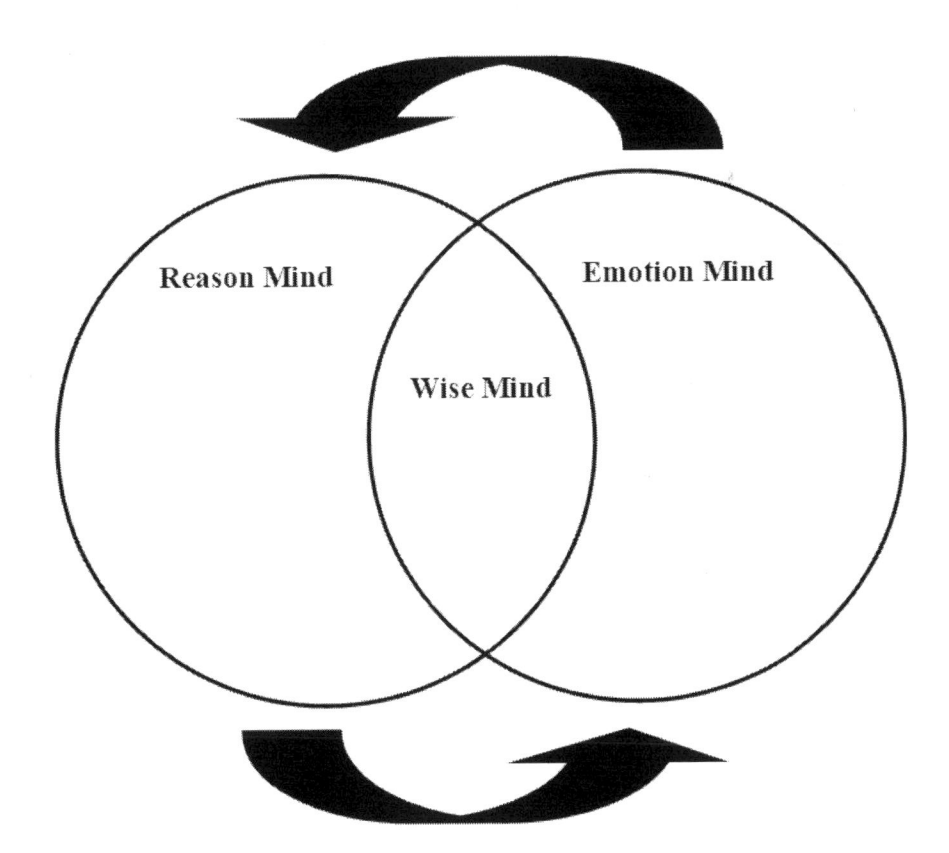

Reason Mind | **Emotion Mind**

Wise Mind

How does the new wise mind statement differ from the original emotion mind statement?

_____

_____

_____

How did your initial emotion mind statement cloud your vision of your reality and impact your emotions/behaviors?

_____

_____

_____

How can you use this technique as you move forward in your recovery?

_____

_____

_____

Week 3

DATE	EXERCISES TO COMPLETE
	Read pages 61-70 and complete exercises: 1-3 and 1-4

OBJECTIVES

- Exploring the roadblocks to recovery when acting out is present.
- Discussing expectations and the purpose of full disclosure.

NOTES – INSIGHTS – THINGS TO EXPLORE IN THERAPY

ACCOUNTABILITY ISSUES – GOALS FOR THE WEEK

PARTNER RECOVERY GROWTH INDEX (PRGI)

DENIAL 1 2 3 4 5 6 7 8 9 10

1 = Believing my partner isn't an addict, denying my partner's progress, and/or denying the hurt and pain I am feeling because of my partner's addiction.

10 = Consistently feeling/expressing the pain caused by my partner's behavior and adjusting boundaries when appropriate due to therapeutic insight and progress.

ANXIETY MANAGEMENT 1 2 3 4 5 6 7 8 9 10

1 = Avoiding anxiety triggers and anxious feelings/sensations in my body

10 = Acknowledging anxiety and using it to provide insight into what is important

ANGER MANAGEMENT 1 2 3 4 5 6 7 8 9 10

1 = Having explosive outbursts, making threats, yelling, stuffing, devaluing, withholding, and other child-like dynamics when experiencing anger

10 = Consistently expressing anger in an adult-to-adult dynamic and externally processing anger via the use of therapeutic tools

DEPRESSION MANAGEMENT 1 2 3 4 5 6 7 8 9 10

1 = Choosing to engage in the victim orientation via avoiding emotional processing, not practicing self-care, and self-loathing every day for the past 7+ days

10 = Consistently choosing to use therapeutic tools, practice self-care, and take behavioral baby steps towards one's mission statement in life every day for the past 14 days

SHAME MANAGEMENT 1 2 3 4 5 6 7 8 9 10

1 = Believing I'm a bad person or a mistake (i.e. I'm a bad wife/I'm unlovable)

10 = Believing I'm a good person who made some mistakes

CO-DEPENDENCY 1 2 3 4 5 6 7 8 9 10

1 = Exhibiting rescuing behavior, failure to set boundaries, failure to implement consequences for boundary failures, and failing to process one's own issues during the past 7+ days.

10 = I have set/executed boundaries, taken behavioral baby steps towards my individual mission statement, acknowledged/processed my emotions, and living a life that is more internally than externally motivated

BOUNDARIES 1 2 3 4 5 6 7 8 9 10

1 = A total lack of boundaries or the use of vague boundaries to justify withholding.

10 = Consistently maintaining boundaries and implementing consequences when boundaries are violated.

TRUST 1 2 3 4 5 6 7 8 9 10

1 = Obsessing about your partner's recovery (OCD/co-dependency/anxiety), ignoring your partner's recovery work (denial/avoidance) and/or doubting your ability to make good decisions in the past 7+ days

10 = Consistently allowing your boundaries/consequences to work for you, expressing emotions in healthy transparent ways during FANOS check-ins and working towards building healthy attachment.

ACTING-IN 1 2 3 4 5 6 7 8 9 10

1 = I withheld emotional/spiritual/physical intimacy in the past 7 days

10 = 6+ months of continuous emotional/spiritual/physical engagement

FORGIVENESS 1 2 3 4 5 6 7 8 9 10

1 = Holding onto anger/resentment/bitterness and refusing to consider forgiveness

10 = I have fully processed my grief, accepted the betrayal, set boundaries, and reached a level of peace due to forgiveness

CONFLICT RESOLUTION 1 2 3 4 5 6 7 8 9 10

1 = Displaying parent-to-child or child-to-child dynamics during conflict or avoiding conflict via people pleasing behaviors

10 = Consistently using healthy assertiveness and active listening with empathy to resolve conflict or reach a compromise in life every day for the past 14 days

SELF-WORTH 1 2 3 4 5 6 7 8 9 10

1 = Feeling/believing I'm inadequate every day in the past 7+ days

10 = Feeling/believing I'm an adequate individual whose worth is not tied to another individual's behavior each day for the past 3+ months

SELF-CARE 1 2 3 4 5 6 7 8 9 10

1 = Neglecting self-care behaviors/No self-care behaviors during the past 7+ days

10 = Consistently practicing self-care behaviors each day for the past year

Roadblocks to Recovery:

1. Lack of commitment/time to work on all aspects of the recovery program.
2. The addict decides to work recovery for his partner to not lose his or her relationship.
3. Lack of full disclosure by the addict to his therapist.
4. Lack of full disclosure by the addict to his partner.
5. The partner does not commit to his or her individual recovery.
6. The partner is co-dependent and/or has unprocessed trauma that if untreated, will keep the relationship from healing.
7. The partner prematurely forgives the addict without allowing himself or herself to go through the grief process.
8. The partner refuses to enforce boundary consequences in the relationship.
9. The addict is working his or her recovery for sexual addiction but failing to work his or her recovery for intimacy anorexia.
10. The partner is refusing to process his or her anger towards his or her addicted partner and is using the anger to keep his or

her partner at a distance despite the addict's therapeutic progress.

11. Neurodevelopmental issues such as Autism Spectrum Disorder (ASD) or Attention Deficit Hyperactivity Disorder (ADHD) are drivers for compulsivity and emotional issues in the relationship.

12. The partner has intimacy anorexia or reactive intimacy anorexia and is unwilling to do the IA dailies to experientially work towards healing in the relationship.

13. Personality Disorders are present in one or both partners and have contributed to the chaos of the addiction cycle without insight into applying what has been learned in therapy. The likely personality disorders are Narcissistic Personality Disorder, Borderline Personality Disorder, Obsessive Compulsive Personality Disorder, Anti-social Personality Disorder, and Schizoid Personality Disorder.

14. Partners have refused to forgive his or her addicted partner but have stayed in the relationship out of dependency.

15. Addicts have refused to forgive themselves despite receiving forgiveness from his or her partner and higher power.

16. Addicts burn themselves out on recovery and gradually "checkout" of doing homework assignments, group work, meetings, and maintaining accountability.

17. Addict struggles to develop empathy for his or her partner's emotional triggers and continues to get defensive when his or her partner experiences a trigger.

18. Addict uses the excuse of spiritual enlightenment or miraculous healing to absolve themselves from having to work his or her recovery like everyone else.

19. Addict has an obvious cooccurring addiction that he or she refuses to address via treatment.

20. Addict fakes recovery by pretending to work his or her program while secretly continuing to act-out.

21. A partner has obsessive compulsive disorder and cannot stop ruminating about his or her partner's addiction and recovery.

22. Unrealistic expectations of recovery and/or relationship recovery.

EXERCISE 1-3: HEALTHY EXPECTATIONS WORKSHEET

Now that you are more familiar with the jargon, treatment methodologies, and timetables associated with recovery, it is important to develop healthy expectations as you begin your recovery journey. Answer the following questions below and process them with your therapist, life coach, and/or group.

What were my individual and relational expectations prior to reading this chapter? What has changed after reading this chapter?

_____

_____

_____

_____

_____

_____

_____

What support do I need from the group to make sure that my expectations remain realistic?

___

What recovery roadblocks may be an issue in my situation?

___

EXERCISE 1-4: PROS/CONS FOR FULL DISCLOSURE

This exercise is designed to help you reflect on the pros and cons of doing full disclosure with your addicted partner. Complete the chart and reflection questions before processing this exercise with your therapist, life coach, and/or group.

PROS AND CONS OF DOING FULL DISCLOSURE	
Pros:	**Cons:**

Take a moment to review your chart. What thoughts and feelings come to mind regarding full disclosure?

On a scale of 1-10, with 10 being I'm completely committed to doing full disclosure and 1 being I'm not committed to doing full disclosure, where would you rate yourself at this time? Explain.

What support would you need if you decided to proceed with full disclosure?

Week 4

DATE	EXERCISES TO COMPLETE
	Read pages 71-91 and complete exercises: 2-1 and 2-2

OBJECTIVES

- Exploring the role of trauma in recovery.
- Develop and implement a self-care plan.
- Exploring the importance of developing a mind-body connection.

NOTES – INSIGHTS – THINGS TO EXPLORE IN THERAPY

_____
_____
_____
_____
_____
_____
_____
_____
_____
_____

ACCOUNTABILITY ISSUES – GOALS FOR THE WEEK

_____
_____
_____
_____
_____
_____
_____
_____
_____
_____
_____

PARTNER RECOVERY GROWTH INDEX (PRGI)

DENIAL 1 2 3 4 5 6 7 8 9 10

1 = Believing my partner isn't an addict, denying my partner's progress, and/or denying the hurt and pain I am feeling because of my partner's addiction.

10 = Consistently feeling/expressing the pain caused by my partner's behavior and adjusting boundaries when appropriate due to therapeutic insight and progress.

ANXIETY MANAGEMENT 1 2 3 4 5 6 7 8 9 10

1 = Avoiding anxiety triggers and anxious feelings/sensations in my body

10 = Acknowledging anxiety and using it to provide insight into what is important

ANGER MANAGEMENT 1 2 3 4 5 6 7 8 9 10

1 = Having explosive outbursts, making threats, yelling, stuffing, devaluing, withholding, and other child-like dynamics when experiencing anger

10 = Consistently expressing anger in an adult-to-adult dynamic and externally processing anger via the use of therapeutic tools

DEPRESSION MANAGEMENT 1 2 3 4 5 6 7 8 9 10

1 = Choosing to engage in the victim orientation via avoiding emotional processing, not practicing self-care, and self-loathing every day for the past 7+ days

10 = Consistently choosing to use therapeutic tools, practice self-care, and take behavioral baby steps towards one's mission statement in life every day for the past 14 days

SHAME MANAGEMENT 1 2 3 4 5 6 7 8 9 10

1 = Believing I'm a bad person or a mistake (i.e. I'm a bad wife/I'm unlovable)

10 = Believing I'm a good person who made some mistakes

CO-DEPENDENCY 1 2 3 4 5 6 7 8 9 10

1 = Exhibiting rescuing behavior, failure to set boundaries, failure to implement consequences for boundary failures, and failing to process one's own issues during the past 7+ days.

10 = I have set/executed boundaries, taken behavioral baby steps towards my individual mission statement, acknowledged/processed my emotions, and living a life that is more internally than externally motivated

BOUNDARIES | 1 2 3 4 5 6 7 8 9 10

1 = A total lack of boundaries or the use of vague boundaries to justify withholding.

10 = Consistently maintaining boundaries and implementing consequences when boundaries are violated.

TRUST | 1 2 3 4 5 6 7 8 9 10

1 = Obsessing about your partner's recovery (OCD/co-dependency/anxiety), ignoring your partner's recovery work (denial/avoidance) and/or doubting your ability to make good decisions in the past 7+ days

10 = Consistently allowing your boundaries/consequences to work for you, expressing emotions in healthy transparent ways during FANOS check-ins and working towards building healthy attachment.

ACTING-IN | 1 2 3 4 5 6 7 8 9 10

1 = I withheld emotional/spiritual/physical intimacy in the past 7 days

10 = 6+ months of continuous emotional/spiritual/physical engagement

FORGIVENESS | 1 2 3 4 5 6 7 8 9 10

1 = Holding onto anger/resentment/bitterness and refusing to consider forgiveness

10 = I have fully processed my grief, accepted the betrayal, set boundaries, and reached a level of peace due to forgiveness

CONFLICT RESOLUTION | 1 2 3 4 5 6 7 8 9 10

1 = Displaying parent-to-child or child-to-child dynamics during conflict or avoiding conflict via people pleasing behaviors

10 = Consistently using healthy assertiveness and active listening with empathy to resolve conflict or reach a compromise in life every day for the past 14 days

SELF-WORTH | 1 2 3 4 5 6 7 8 9 10

1 = Feeling/believing I'm inadequate every day in the past 7+ days

10 = Feeling/believing I'm an adequate individual whose worth is not tied to another individual's behavior each day for the past 3+ months

SELF-CARE | 1 2 3 4 5 6 7 8 9 10

1 = Neglecting self-care behaviors/No self-care behaviors during the past 7+ days

10 = Consistently practicing self-care behaviors each day for the past year

Chapter 2: Understanding the Role of Trauma within Addiction and Partner's Recovery

Many of us are familiar with the expression of "putting the cart before the horse." In the time of horse and buggies, this idiom created visual imagery that people could logically understand. Horse drawn carriages were the norm and the idea of having a horse push a load versus pulling a load was irrational due to the loss of leverage by a horse's legs. The inability of a horse to push a cart isn't the horse's fault. A horse has amazing power and strength when harnessed with a cart in the proper sequence. Understanding the proper sequence and applying those principles is the difference between a productive relationship between the horse and cart and a relationship that gets stuck in the mud. This expression has application to individual and marital recovery regarding trauma and addiction. For the spouse of an addict, attempting to heal the relationship before individually addressing the trauma of disclosure via therapeutic processing and the establishment of boundaries is putting the cart before the horse. For the addict, attempting to heal the relationship before failing to work your recovery, establish sobriety, address your own traumatic past, and empathetically respond to your partner's triggers via intensive therapy is also putting the cart before the horse. Individual recovery for the partner and addict is imperative to the proper sequence of therapeutic growth. Unfortunately, trauma, anxiety, distress, fears of abandonment, dependency, co-dependency, feelings of inadequacy all drive the idea of fixing the relationship before individual healing. Such an approach is often the product of denial regarding the gravity of the situation and the desire to move forward without experiencing appropriate negative emotions/grief. This is clinically a mistake because it can create more harm to the individual and the relationship due to trauma-related behaviors exhibited between the partner and addict while attempting to process the trauma in a fight or flight state.

Let's examine the neuroscience behind this process in the following diagram:

Neuroscience of Anxiety

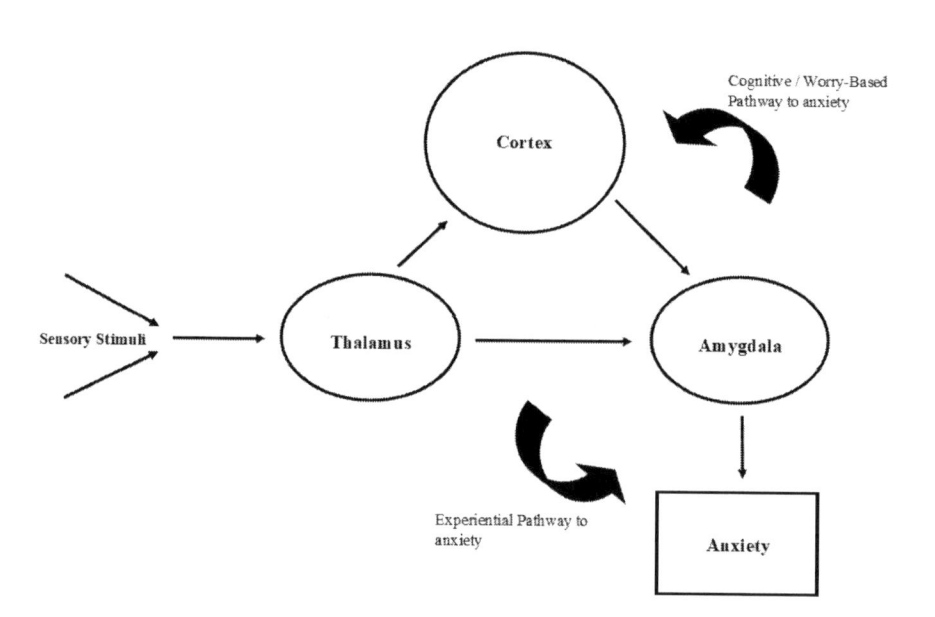

```
                    Cortex
                                    ← Cognitive / Worry-Based
                                      Pathway to anxiety

Sensory Stimuli  →  Thalamus  →  Amygdala

                 Experiential Pathway to
                 anxiety                  Anxiety
```

The amygdala and cortex play major roles in the experience/processing of anxiety in the body and brain. The human brain is constantly taking in sensory stimuli from the environment. Sensory stimuli are things we see, smell, taste, touch, feel, and hear. Most of the data goes into the Thalamus, which sends the information to the Cerebral Cortex and your Amygdalae. While the Cortex is responsible for executive processing, emotions, and cognitive decision making, your Amygdalae are responsible for regulating your response to dangerous stimuli. In our bodies, we have a sympathetic nervous system and parasympathetic nervous system. Both nervous systems are autonomous, meaning they regulate themselves without you having to consciously think about it. Your Amygdala assists in stimulating the sympathetic system to illicit a fight or flight response to dangerous experiential stimuli. On the other side of the coin, your parasympathetic nervous system regulates your calming response. With trauma, the issue between the two systems is due to the speed of transfer of trauma-related stimuli from the Thalamus to the respective Cortex and Amygdala. The Amygdala gets the data first and can trigger a fight or flight response before the Cortex has a chance to activate the calming use of the parasympathetic nervous system. In essence, the Amygdala triggers a response before the Cortex has time regulate it. Let's look at this through an example of a car accident. When a person gets into an accident, the following multiple sensory stimuli are present:

Sight: blur of cars/trucks, vehicle damage, blood, broken glass, intersection/roads, medical personnel, bystanders

Sound: squealing wheels, breaking glass, screams, horn, collision, etc.

Smell: gas, fire, oil, radiator fluid, smoke, burnt rubber, etc.

Taste: blood, sweat, smoke, etc.

Touch/Feelings: anxiety, panic, terror, pain, sadness, etc.

These are only a fraction of the sensory stimuli associated with the trauma of a car accident, but you can see how this information is relayed to the Amygdala to illicit a fight or flight response surrounding the danger of driving. Prior to the accident, you likely had hundreds if not thousands of hours of driving without that type of fear. However, the sensory stimuli of the accident created an experiential response of fear/anxiety related to driving. For those of you who have ever been in a significant automobile accident, you know that it probably took some time to get over your anxiety surrounding driving in certain areas where the accident occurred or perhaps driving at all. In summary, it took you forcing yourself to face the fear via the experience of driving and using your Cortex to tell your Amygdala that driving wasn't always going to end in an accident to reprogram the Amygdala to encode the message that driving was relatively safe. If we replace the car accident scenario with the trauma of disclosure of your partners acting out behavior, what sensory stimuli might be present? Consider the following list:

Sight: your partner's suspicious behavior leading up to discovery/disclosure, images of pornography you found on his or her phone/tablet/computer, text messages/apps found on his or her phone, images of acting out partners on social media, certain hotels or locations where acting out behavior took place, your partner's behaviors or facial expressions when talking about his or her acting out behavior, sex scenes in movies/media, seeing your partner stare at other people in public, seeing your partner interact with other people in flirtatious ways, seeing your partner quickly put his or her phone down when you walk in the room, etc.

Sound: the sound of pornography, the sound of physical intimacy, yelling/gaslighting when confronting your partner over their past acting out behavior, the sound of your partner's phone receiving a text message or call, your partner gaslighting you or getting angry at you when you challenged them when triggered, etc.

Smell: the smell of physical intimacy, unknown perfume/cologne, your partner's perfume/cologne after they returned from acting out, food you were cooking/eating at the time of discovery, etc.

Taste: Food you were cooking/eating at the time of discovery, wine that you drank to numb your pain after discovery/disclosure, etc.

Touch/Feelings: physical intimacy and/or certain behaviors/positions, physical touch, anxiety, anger, resentment, panic, disgust, rage, abandonment, rejection, nausea, sadness, depression, inadequacy, self-doubt, fear, powerlessness, helplessness, shame, depression, etc.

As you can see from this illustration, your partner, sex, and everyday experiences can become trauma triggers after the discovery/disclosure of acting out behavior. Attempting to heal the relationship without first addressing the trauma-related neuroscience issues in a therapeutic setting is futile because your brain and body are telling you that your partner is a threat. While this is a healthy response in the beginning of the process due to his or her betrayal/infidelity, it is not a healthy response to maintain for the rest of the relationship if your goal is reconciliation. The timetable of this process is subjective and specific to the level of trauma experienced by the partner pre and post discovery/disclosure. This also includes childhood and other relational trauma that you may have experienced prior to meeting your partner.

Our program is designed to assist clients in helping their amygdalae heal via experiential treatment. Once the amygdalae begin to regulate, it becomes easier to apply what you have learned in recovery and adapt your old behavior to new behavior. Such an approach is necessary, because an individual's brain in fight-or-flight is reducing the ability of the cortex to function at an optimum state. This reduction allows the brain to overcompensate for the sympathetic nervous system which takes over via fight-or-flight behaviors (survival instincts). The issue with this process is the cortex is responsible for executive functioning (complex math, theoretical reasoning, etc.). Thus, the reduction in cognitive ability during a hypervigilant/fight-or-flight state is typical and makes learning new behaviors difficult. Understanding this process is critical to your recovery due to trauma created by your partner's addictive behaviors. Despite the emotional swings, explosive anger, immobilizing sadness, heart palpitating anxiety, and potential out-of-body experiences, you are not crazy. At this point in the reading, you are probably starting to connect the dots that your body is in a state of trauma-induced hypervigilance (the state of fight or flight making you sensitive to any feelings, sights, sounds, or even smells associated with the trauma). This arousal state has been genetically encoded within you to protect you in dangerous situations and help you identify future threats. However, it is likely becoming clear that one of the triggers for your trauma is someone you love. As you can see, this paradox requires treatment that understands the neuroscience behind your trauma and can assist in giving you the tools to establish an environment of safety before true therapeutic healing can begin.

If you have a traumatic past prior to your relationship with your partner, or if you have neurodevelopmental issues, this process can be more complex and therapeutic progress may take more time. If this sounds like you, make sure you discuss this with your individual therapist to ensure that those elements are included in your treatment plan. You may need to develop an EMDR treatment plan or additional forms of experiential therapy to address your trauma needs.

The following trauma processing exercises can generate a plethora of emotions. Good trauma work requires a healthy balance of self-care because it can be emotionally depleting. It is imperative that you are taking care of yourself and connecting with your support network as you process the exercises. It is not abnormal for partners of individuals who struggle with sexual acting out/acting in behavior to experience feelings of inadequacy and depression. This is often because of the sense of powerlessness, secrecy, betrayal, and comparison associated with the acting out/acting in behavior. You are not inadequate, and it is important for you to fight for yourself. Your depression and feelings of inadequacy will tell you that your experience is hopeless, and you are too tired or overwhelmed to function. While you may be emotionally exhausted, practicing self-care is the first step to breaking through your depression and showing yourself that YOU ARE ENOUGH and YOU ARE WORTH IT. Let's get started!

EXERCISE 2-1: DEVELOPING A SELF-CARE PLAN

In this exercise, you will develop a self-care plan. It is imperative that this plan is implemented with consistency to avoid psychological depletion. Your ability to implement this plan will also be tracked in your weekly Partner Recovery Growth Index.

> **Journaling:** Journaling is the process of identifying your emotions and processing them via writing. While everyone doesn't enjoy journaling, the lack of journaling in partner's recovery is often a product of emotional avoidance. Thus, consistent journaling is imperative to the recovery process. If you struggle with journaling, use the feelings wheel included in this book to assist in the identification of your emotions.
>
> I agree to journal _____ X for _____ minutes each week.

> **Mindfulness:** Mindfulness is the process of being 100% present (physically and emotionally) in the moment. Individuals struggling with anxiety or emotional stuffing often struggle with being mindfully present in daily life. While most people think of

mindfulness via yoga or meditation, you can also practice mindfulness while taking a walk or sipping a cup of coffee if you are 100% connected to the experience. Mindfulness can also be used to identify emotions by focusing on the somatic sensations you are experiencing and internally asking yourself what the sensations are attempting to emotionally communicate to you. If you struggle with being overwhelmed and lack enjoyment in life or if you struggle with experiencing task-related tunnel vision, we challenge you to incorporate mindfulness into your self-care treatment plan.

I agree to practice mindfulness by _____

_____ for _____ minutes _____ X each week.

Exercise: While exercising has many physical benefits, it is also a great way to process anger, anxiety, stress, and depression. If you notice your body experiencing a lot of tension, physical activity is a great way to release that tension.

I agree to exercise for _____ minutes _____ X each week. I will accomplish this via the activities of _____

_____
_____
_____
_____

Connection: Human beings have an innate desire for connection. Addiction creates an environment of isolation and for a partner, the emotional disconnection from an addict and the social/emotional disconnection due to the emotional turmoil of discovery/disclosure can leave a person withdrawing from connection. Healthy connection in partner's recovery is all about support, bonding, processing emotions, having fun, and accountability. For this portion of your self-care plan, select multiple people whom you are willing to connect with daily, weekly, bi-weekly, etc. via phone conversations and spending time together. Consider adding some of the people from this group to your self-care connection plan.

(Name of Person 1):_____

I will call _____ for _____ minutes _____ X each

_____.

(Name of Person 2):_____

I will call _____ for _____ minutes _____ X each

_____.

(Name of Person 3):_____

I will call _____ for _____ minutes _____ X each

_____.

(Name of Person 5):_____

I will call _____ for _____ minutes _____ X each

_____.

(Name of Person 6):_____

I will call _____ for _____ minutes _____ X each

_____.

(Name of Person 7):_____

I will call _____ for _____ minutes _____ X each

_____.

(Name of Person 8):_____

I will call _____ for _____ minutes _____ X each

_____.

(Name of Person 9):_____

I will call _____ for _____ minutes _____ X each

_____.

(Name of Person 10):_____

I will call _____ for _____ minutes _____ X each _____.

Spirituality: Connection to a Higher Power is important to recovery as it connects us to the idea that it will take a power greater than ourselves to overcome obstacles created by addiction. Whether your Higher Power is Jesus Christ, Buddha, your support group, etc., take time to pray, meditate, and connect with your higher power, seeking insight, strength, purpose, healing, and a relinquishing of unhealthy control in your recovery.

I will connect with my Higher Power by _____, _____ X each week. _____, _____ X each week. _____, _____ X each week.

EXERCISE 2-2: IDENTIFYING TRAUMA SYMPTOMS

What are some of the emotions you have been experiencing due to the trauma of your partner's acting-out/acting-in behavior?

_____

_____

_____

_____

_____

What are some of the bodily sensations you have noticed due to the discovery of your partner's acting-out/acting-in behavior?

_____

_____

_____

_____

_____

When you reflect on your feelings and bodily sensations associated with your trauma, what particular triggers come to mind? (i.e. sights, smells, sounds, etc.)

Week 5

DATE	EXERCISES TO COMPLETE
	Review pages 92-101 and complete exercises: 2-3 and 2-4

OBJECTIVES

- Connecting the mind/body to specific trauma triggers.
- Group processing of insights related to trauma triggers.

NOTES – INSIGHTS – THINGS TO EXPLORE IN THERAPY

_____
_____
_____
_____
_____
_____
_____
_____
_____

ACCOUNTABILITY ISSUES – GOALS FOR THE WEEK

_____
_____
_____
_____
_____
_____
_____
_____
_____
_____

PARTNER RECOVERY GROWTH INDEX (PRGI)

DENIAL 1 2 3 4 5 6 7 8 9 10

1 = Believing my partner isn't an addict, denying my partner's progress, and/or denying the hurt and pain I am feeling because of my partner's addiction.

10 = Consistently feeling/expressing the pain caused by my partner's behavior and adjusting boundaries when appropriate due to therapeutic insight and progress.

ANXIETY MANAGEMENT 1 2 3 4 5 6 7 8 9 10

1 = Avoiding anxiety triggers and anxious feelings/sensations in my body

10 = Acknowledging anxiety and using it to provide insight into what is important

ANGER MANAGEMENT 1 2 3 4 5 6 7 8 9 10

1 = Having explosive outbursts, making threats, yelling, stuffing, devaluing, withholding, and other child-like dynamics when experiencing anger

10 = Consistently expressing anger in an adult-to-adult dynamic and externally processing anger via the use of therapeutic tools

DEPRESSION MANAGEMENT 1 2 3 4 5 6 7 8 9 10

1 = Choosing to engage in the victim orientation via avoiding emotional processing, not practicing self-care, and self-loathing every day for the past 7+ days

10 = Consistently choosing to use therapeutic tools, practice self-care, and take behavioral baby steps towards one's mission statement in life every day for the past 14 days

SHAME MANAGEMENT 1 2 3 4 5 6 7 8 9 10

1 = Believing I'm a bad person or a mistake (i.e. I'm a bad wife/I'm unlovable)

10 = Believing I'm a good person who made some mistakes

CO-DEPENDENCY 1 2 3 4 5 6 7 8 9 10

1 = Exhibiting rescuing behavior, failure to set boundaries, failure to implement consequences for boundary failures, and failing to process one's own issues during the past 7+ days.

10 = I have set/executed boundaries, taken behavioral baby steps towards my individual mission statement, acknowledged/processed my emotions, and living a life that is more internally than externally motivated

BOUNDARIES | 1 2 3 4 5 6 7 8 9 10

1 = A total lack of boundaries or the use of vague boundaries to justify withholding.

10 = Consistently maintaining boundaries and implementing consequences when boundaries are violated.

TRUST | 1 2 3 4 5 6 7 8 9 10

1 = Obsessing about your partner's recovery (OCD/co-dependency/anxiety), ignoring your partner's recovery work (denial/avoidance) and/or doubting your ability to make good decisions in the past 7+ days

10 = Consistently allowing your boundaries/consequences to work for you, expressing emotions in healthy transparent ways during FANOS check-ins and working towards building healthy attachment.

ACTING-IN | 1 2 3 4 5 6 7 8 9 10

1 = I withheld emotional/spiritual/physical intimacy in the past 7 days

10 = 6+ months of continuous emotional/spiritual/physical engagement

FORGIVENESS | 1 2 3 4 5 6 7 8 9 10

1 = Holding onto anger/resentment/bitterness and refusing to consider forgiveness

10 = I have fully processed my grief, accepted the betrayal, set boundaries, and reached a level of peace due to forgiveness

CONFLICT RESOLUTION | 1 2 3 4 5 6 7 8 9 10

1 = Displaying parent-to-child or child-to-child dynamics during conflict or avoiding conflict via people pleasing behaviors

10 = Consistently using healthy assertiveness and active listening with empathy to resolve conflict or reach a compromise in life every day for the past 14 days

SELF-WORTH | 1 2 3 4 5 6 7 8 9 10

1 = Feeling/believing I'm inadequate every day in the past 7+ days

10 = Feeling/believing I'm an adequate individual whose worth is not tied to another individual's behavior each day for the past 3+ months

SELF-CARE | 1 2 3 4 5 6 7 8 9 10

1 = Neglecting self-care behaviors/No self-care behaviors during the past 7+ days

10 = Consistently practicing self-care behaviors each day for the past year

EXERCISE 2-3: MAPPING TRAUMA TRIGGERS

Now that you have begun to identify the what, where, and why concerning your trauma triggers, let's map their associations together. In the space below, use shapes or symbols to identify 15 triggers associated with your partner's acting out/acting in behaviors. Make sure you space out multiple triggers across each page. Then, draw lines to emotions associated with each trigger and where you feel that emotion in your body. If you run out of room, feel free to use a large piece of paper to map your triggers. The key is to establish a mind/body connection with each trigger.

Example:

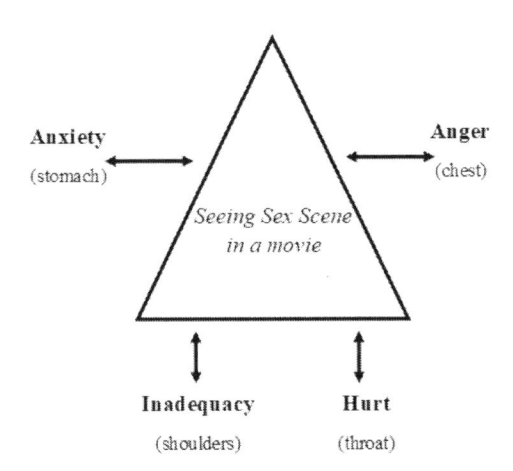

```
            Anxiety              Anger
           (stomach)            (chest)
              ↔   ╱▲╲   ↔
                 ╱   ╲
                ╱Seeing Sex Scene╲
               ╱   in a movie    ╲
              ╱_____╲
                  ↕         ↕
              Inadequacy   Hurt
              (shoulders) (throat)
```

EXERCISE 2-3: MAPPING TRAUMA TRIGGERS

EXERCISE 2-3: MAPPING TRAUMA TRIGGERS

EXERCISE 2-3: MAPPING TRAUMA TRIGGERS

EXERCISE 2-4: REFLECTIONS ON YOUR TRAUMA TRIGGERS MAP

Refer to this exercise for your boundaries work in chapter 3

1. Now that you have visually mapped your trauma triggers, what themes do you notice as you look at your exercise?

_____

_____

_____

_____

_____

2. What emotions are you struggling with concerning the trauma triggers in your life?

_____

_____

_____

_____

_____

_____

3. What do you need to cope with these emotions in healthy ways? In what ways are you using unhealthy coping methods?

4. What triggers can be addressed by developing boundaries in your relationship with your partner?

_____
_____
_____
_____
_____
_____
_____

Refer to this exercise for your boundaries work in chapter 3

Week 6

DATE	EXERCISES TO COMPLETE
	Read pages 102-118 and complete exercises: 2-5 and 2-6

OBJECTIVES

- Exploring the role of the inner-child in recovery.
- Exploring insights from connecting with your inner-child.
- Group processing of your trauma timeline.

NOTES – INSIGHTS – THINGS TO EXPLORE IN THERAPY

ACCOUNTABILITY ISSUES – GOALS FOR THE WEEK

PARTNER RECOVERY GROWTH INDEX (PRGI)

DENIAL 1 2 3 4 5 6 7 8 9 10

1 = Believing my partner isn't an addict, denying my partner's progress, and/or denying the hurt and pain I am feeling because of my partner's addiction.

10 = Consistently feeling/expressing the pain caused by my partner's behavior and adjusting boundaries when appropriate due to therapeutic insight and progress.

ANXIETY MANAGEMENT 1 2 3 4 5 6 7 8 9 10

1 = Avoiding anxiety triggers and anxious feelings/sensations in my body

10 = Acknowledging anxiety and using it to provide insight into what is important

ANGER MANAGEMENT 1 2 3 4 5 6 7 8 9 10

1 = Having explosive outbursts, making threats, yelling, stuffing, devaluing, withholding, and other child-like dynamics when experiencing anger

10 = Consistently expressing anger in an adult-to-adult dynamic and externally processing anger via the use of therapeutic tools

DEPRESSION MANAGEMENT 1 2 3 4 5 6 7 8 9 10

1 = Choosing to engage in the victim orientation via avoiding emotional processing, not practicing self-care, and self-loathing every day for the past 7+ days

10 = Consistently choosing to use therapeutic tools, practice self-care, and take behavioral baby steps towards one's mission statement in life every day for the past 14 days

SHAME MANAGEMENT 1 2 3 4 5 6 7 8 9 10

1 = Believing I'm a bad person or a mistake (i.e. I'm a bad wife/I'm unlovable)

10 = Believing I'm a good person who made some mistakes

CO-DEPENDENCY 1 2 3 4 5 6 7 8 9 10

1 = Exhibiting rescuing behavior, failure to set boundaries, failure to implement consequences for boundary failures, and failing to process one's own issues during the past 7+ days.

10 = I have set/executed boundaries, taken behavioral baby steps towards my individual mission statement, acknowledged/processed my emotions, and living a life that is more internally than externally motivated

BOUNDARIES | 1 2 3 4 5 6 7 8 9 10

1 = A total lack of boundaries or the use of vague boundaries to justify withholding.

10 = Consistently maintaining boundaries and implementing consequences when boundaries are violated.

TRUST | 1 2 3 4 5 6 7 8 9 10

1 = Obsessing about your partner's recovery (OCD/co-dependency/anxiety), ignoring your partner's recovery work (denial/avoidance) and/or doubting your ability to make good decisions in the past 7+ days

10 = Consistently allowing your boundaries/consequences to work for you, expressing emotions in healthy transparent ways during FANOS check-ins and working towards building healthy attachment.

ACTING-IN | 1 2 3 4 5 6 7 8 9 10

1 = I withheld emotional/spiritual/physical intimacy in the past 7 days

10 = 6+ months of continuous emotional/spiritual/physical engagement

FORGIVENESS | 1 2 3 4 5 6 7 8 9 10

1 = Holding onto anger/resentment/bitterness and refusing to consider forgiveness

10 = I have fully processed my grief, accepted the betrayal, set boundaries, and reached a level of peace due to forgiveness

CONFLICT RESOLUTION | 1 2 3 4 5 6 7 8 9 10

1 = Displaying parent-to-child or child-to-child dynamics during conflict or avoiding conflict via people pleasing behaviors

10 = Consistently using healthy assertiveness and active listening with empathy to resolve conflict or reach a compromise in life every day for the past 14 days

SELF-WORTH | 1 2 3 4 5 6 7 8 9 10

1 = Feeling/believing I'm inadequate every day in the past 7+ days

10 = Feeling/believing I'm an adequate individual whose worth is not tied to another individual's behavior each day for the past 3+ months

SELF-CARE | 1 2 3 4 5 6 7 8 9 10

1 = Neglecting self-care behaviors/No self-care behaviors during the past 7+ days

10 = Consistently practicing self-care behaviors each day for the past year

In the *Important Concepts* section of this text, we introduced you to **Transactional Analysis Treatment (TA)** – that focuses on the internal family system (IFS) between the inner parent, inner adult, and inner child of an individual. TA explores how the parent-adult-child (PAC) interacts with other parent-adult-child (PAC) dynamics within the self and in external relationships. When dealing with trauma in our present relationships, an individual can emotionally and somatically experience inner-child wounds from past childhood experiences. Remember when learning about the neuroscience of anxiety? Sensory stimuli trigger experiential anxiety-induced responses in the sympathetic and parasympathetic nervous systems. Thus, our inner-adult is impacted by the emotional pain of our inner-child. When this happens, the inner-child influences behavior with coping skills learned as a child. Sometimes a child is forced to use self-taught coping methods due to neglect, abuse, or lack of modeling. This is often the case in the development of acting out/acting in behavior and is possibly playing a role in your partner's individual struggles. However, understanding your own inner-child triggers is critical to your ability to healthily attach in your relationship and process the trauma of your partner's betrayal.

EXERCISE 2-5: CONNECTING TO YOUR INNER-CHILD

The following exercise can be emotionally triggering and will take some time in a quiet, undisturbed location to complete. If you are unsure of your ability to cope with potential emotional flooding, we encourage you to process this exercise individually with your therapist before processing the exercise in group.

Step 1: Take a seat in a comfortable chair and slow your breathing.

Step 2: Turn to exercise 2.3 in your Recovery Journal.

Step 3: Number your top 10 triggers by ranking them 1 through 10 with 10 being the least distressing and 1 being the most distressing.

Step 4: Focus on a singular mapped trauma trigger and allow the emotions of the trigger to surface as you focus on the most distressing parts of the trigger.

Step 5: Internally ask yourself, what does this trauma trigger say about me?

Step 6: Close your eyes and focus on what is going on in your body as you reflect on the question of what the trigger says about you.

Step 7: Internally ask the bodily sensations what they are trying to tell you (give them permission).

Step 8: Internally ask yourself, when was the first time you remember feeling this way in your life.

Step 9: Open your eyes and journal your insights in the space provided.

Step 10: Repeat steps 4-9 on your remaining mapped triggers until you have processed your top 10 most distressing triggers.

Step 11: Once you have documented everything, close your eyes and focus on your inner child. Tell him or her that you love him or her and that you are sorry for all that he or she has experienced in his or her life. Now ask your inner child if they would allow your inner adult to come into the room to take control and apply what has been learned today.

Trauma Trigger 1: _____

    Negative belief about myself: _____

    Age when this belief began in my life: _____

    Circumstances surrounding the origins of this belief: _____

_____

_____

_____

_____

    Emotions present during this processing experience: _____

_____

_____

    Notes and insights for therapeutic processing: _____

_____

_____

_____

_____

Trauma Trigger 2: _____

    Negative belief about myself: _____

    Age when this belief began in my life: _____

    Circumstances surrounding the origins of this belief: _____

_____

_____

_____

_____

    Emotions present during this processing experience: _____

_____

_____

    Notes and insights for therapeutic processing: _____

_____

_____

_____

_____

Trauma Trigger 3: _____

    Negative belief about myself: _____

    Age when this belief began in my life: _____

    Circumstances surrounding the origins of this belief: _____

_____

_____

_____

_____

    Emotions present during this processing experience: _____

_____

_____

    Notes and insights for therapeutic processing: _____

_____

_____

_____

_____

Trauma Trigger 4: _____

    Negative belief about myself: _____

    Age when this belief began in my life: _____

    Circumstances surrounding the origins of this belief: _____

_____

_____

_____

_____

    Emotions present during this processing experience: _____

_____

_____

    Notes and insights for therapeutic processing: _____

_____

_____

_____

_____

Trauma Trigger 5: _____

    Negative belief about myself: _____

    Age when this belief began in my life: _____

    Circumstances surrounding the origins of this belief: _____

_____

_____

_____

_____

    Emotions present during this processing experience: _____

_____

_____

    Notes and insights for therapeutic processing: _____

_____

_____

_____

_____

Trauma Trigger 6: _____

    Negative belief about myself: _____

    Age when this belief began in my life: _____

    Circumstances surrounding the origins of this belief: _____

_____

_____

_____

_____

    Emotions present during this processing experience: _____

_____

_____

    Notes and insights for therapeutic processing: _____

_____

_____

_____

_____

Trauma Trigger 7: _____

    Negative belief about myself: _____

    Age when this belief began in my life: _____

    Circumstances surrounding the origins of this belief: _____

_____

_____

_____

_____

    Emotions present during this processing experience: _____

_____

_____

    Notes and insights for therapeutic processing: _____

_____

_____

_____

_____

Trauma Trigger 8: _____

    Negative belief about myself: _____

    Age when this belief began in my life: _____

    Circumstances surrounding the origins of this belief: _____

_____

_____

_____

_____

    Emotions present during this processing experience: _____

_____

_____

    Notes and insights for therapeutic processing: _____

_____

_____

_____

_____

Trauma Trigger 9: _____

    Negative belief about myself: _____

    Age when this belief began in my life: _____

    Circumstances surrounding the origins of this belief: _____

_____

_____

_____

_____

    Emotions present during this processing experience: _____

_____

_____

    Notes and insights for therapeutic processing: _____

_____

_____

_____

_____

Trauma Trigger 10: _____

    Negative belief about myself: _____

    Age when this belief began in my life: _____

    Circumstances surrounding the origins of this belief: _____

_____

_____

_____

_____

    Emotions present during this processing experience: _____

_____

_____

    Notes and insights for therapeutic processing: _____

_____

_____

_____

_____

EXERCISE 2-6: CREATING A TRAUMA TIMELINE

In the space below, you will develop a trauma timeline. In the previous exercise, you identified 10 triggering experiences that may or may not have origins with the trauma of your partner's betrayal. It is important to identify all of impactful experiences that have occurred across your lifespan. On the timeline below, place a dot at the appropriate age each event occurred and label the dot with a brief description of the event (i.e. parents divorced, sexual abuse, discovered partner's acting-out behavior, etc.). You will also want to fill in the gaps with events that were significant to you that didn't surface during **EXERCISE 2-5: CONNECTING TO YOUR INNER-CHILD**. If you need more room, use a larger piece of paper to draw out your timeline. It is critical that you do not minimize your traumatic experiences as this timeline is an opportunity for YOU to tell YOUR story.

Birth   **Today**

Week 7

DATE	EXERCISES TO COMPLETE
	Read pages 119-125 and complete exercise: 2-7

OBJECTIVES

- Reviewing the importance of self-care and self-acceptance when processing trauma in recovery work.
- Group processing of letters to your inner-child.

NOTES – INSIGHTS – THINGS TO EXPLORE IN THERAPY

_____
_____
_____
_____
_____
_____
_____
_____
_____
_____

ACCOUNTABILITY ISSUES – GOALS FOR THE WEEK

_____
_____
_____
_____
_____
_____
_____
_____
_____
_____
_____

PARTNER RECOVERY GROWTH INDEX (PRGI)

DENIAL 1 2 3 4 5 6 7 8 9 10

1 = Believing my partner isn't an addict, denying my partner's progress, and/or denying the hurt and pain I am feeling because of my partner's addiction.

10 = Consistently feeling/expressing the pain caused by my partner's behavior and adjusting boundaries when appropriate due to therapeutic insight and progress.

ANXIETY MANAGEMENT 1 2 3 4 5 6 7 8 9 10

1 = Avoiding anxiety triggers and anxious feelings/sensations in my body

10 = Acknowledging anxiety and using it to provide insight into what is important

ANGER MANAGEMENT 1 2 3 4 5 6 7 8 9 10

1 = Having explosive outbursts, making threats, yelling, stuffing, devaluing, withholding, and other child-like dynamics when experiencing anger

10 = Consistently expressing anger in an adult-to-adult dynamic and externally processing anger via the use of therapeutic tools

DEPRESSION MANAGEMENT 1 2 3 4 5 6 7 8 9 10

1 = Choosing to engage in the victim orientation via avoiding emotional processing, not practicing self-care, and self-loathing every day for the past 7+ days

10 = Consistently choosing to use therapeutic tools, practice self-care, and take behavioral baby steps towards one's mission statement in life every day for the past 14 days

SHAME MANAGEMENT 1 2 3 4 5 6 7 8 9 10

1 = Believing I'm a bad person or a mistake (i.e. I'm a bad wife/I'm unlovable)

10 = Believing I'm a good person who made some mistakes

CO-DEPENDENCY 1 2 3 4 5 6 7 8 9 10

1 = Exhibiting rescuing behavior, failure to set boundaries, failure to implement consequences for boundary failures, and failing to process one's own issues during the past 7+ days.

10 = I have set/executed boundaries, taken behavioral baby steps towards my individual mission statement, acknowledged/processed my emotions, and living a life that is more internally than externally motivated

BOUNDARIES | 1 2 3 4 5 6 7 8 9 10

1 = A total lack of boundaries or the use of vague boundaries to justify withholding.

10 = Consistently maintaining boundaries and implementing consequences when boundaries are violated.

TRUST | 1 2 3 4 5 6 7 8 9 10

1 = Obsessing about your partner's recovery (OCD/co-dependency/anxiety), ignoring your partner's recovery work (denial/avoidance) and/or doubting your ability to make good decisions in the past 7+ days

10 = Consistently allowing your boundaries/consequences to work for you, expressing emotions in healthy transparent ways during FANOS check-ins and working towards building healthy attachment.

ACTING-IN | 1 2 3 4 5 6 7 8 9 10

1 = I withheld emotional/spiritual/physical intimacy in the past 7 days

10 = 6+ months of continuous emotional/spiritual/physical engagement

FORGIVENESS | 1 2 3 4 5 6 7 8 9 10

1 = Holding onto anger/resentment/bitterness and refusing to consider forgiveness

10 = I have fully processed my grief, accepted the betrayal, set boundaries, and reached a level of peace due to forgiveness

CONFLICT RESOLUTION | 1 2 3 4 5 6 7 8 9 10

1 = Displaying parent-to-child or child-to-child dynamics during conflict or avoiding conflict via people pleasing behaviors

10 = Consistently using healthy assertiveness and active listening with empathy to resolve conflict or reach a compromise in life every day for the past 14 days

SELF-WORTH | 1 2 3 4 5 6 7 8 9 10

1 = Feeling/believing I'm inadequate every day in the past 7+ days

10 = Feeling/believing I'm an adequate individual whose worth is not tied to another individual's behavior each day for the past 3+ months

SELF-CARE | 1 2 3 4 5 6 7 8 9 10

1 = Neglecting self-care behaviors/No self-care behaviors during the past 7+ days

10 = Consistently practicing self-care behaviors each day for the past year

Internal insight and **empathy for your wounded inner-child** are critical components following the extensive work you have started in the previous exercises. Sometimes this process uncovers compartmentalized pain, grief, sadness, and fear that have been internally avoided, rationalized, or projected onto yourself or others. These dynamics can lead to unhealthy attachment to yourself and others due to the internal emotional avoidance of what you have experienced in life. These patterns do not mean that you are weak or are a bad person (this belief propagates shame). These patterns simply mean that you have experienced emotional, physical, or psychological trauma, regardless of scale, that have led to the psychological coping patterns of your inner-child who did the best he or she could to survive and make sense of life. We will discuss and explore a greater understanding of those coping patterns in the next section of reading but for now, it is imperative that you focus on seeing your inner-child from a perspective of love, empathy, and compassion. Sometimes clients find doing this hard or difficult due to the presence of misguided coping patterns that create self-loathing and a dislike of the inner-child. If you find yourself experiencing significant resistance, discuss this with your therapist or life coach.

EXERCISE 2-7: WRITE A LETTER TO YOUR INNER CHILD

Now that exercise 2-5 has assisted you in identifying your own inner-child, it is important to recognize the role he or she plays in your everyday life. It is imperative to acknowledge that he or she is a part of you, and he or she is not to be hated, persecuted, or shamed. He or she gets to be loved by you and nurtured to a place of healing and integration via healthy attachment with your inner adult. In this exercise, write a letter to your younger self who experienced the painful things that have been reopened by the trauma of your present-day relationship to an addict. Say all the unsaid things you wish had been said to him or her from a position of nurturing and love.

Dear _____,

_____

_____

_____

_____

_____

_____

_____

_____

_____

_____

_____

_____

With all of my love, _____ .

What emotions and insights surfaced as you wrote this letter:

_____

_____

_____

_____

_____

_____

Week 8

DATE	EXERCISES TO COMPLETE
	Read pages 126-141 and complete exercises: 2-8A, 2-8B, and 2-9

OBJECTIVES

- Exploring the role of parts in partner's recovery.
- Group processing of the parts timeline and exploration of how life experiences influence the behaviors of parts.

NOTES – INSIGHTS – THINGS TO EXPLORE IN THERAPY

_____
_____
_____
_____
_____
_____
_____
_____
_____
_____

ACCOUNTABILITY ISSUES – GOALS FOR THE WEEK

_____
_____
_____
_____
_____
_____
_____
_____
_____
_____

PARTNER RECOVERY GROWTH INDEX (PRGI)

DENIAL 1 2 3 4 5 6 7 8 9 10

1 = Believing my partner isn't an addict, denying my partner's progress, and/or denying the hurt and pain I am feeling because of my partner's addiction.

10 = Consistently feeling/expressing the pain caused by my partner's behavior and adjusting boundaries when appropriate due to therapeutic insight and progress.

ANXIETY MANAGEMENT 1 2 3 4 5 6 7 8 9 10

1 = Avoiding anxiety triggers and anxious feelings/sensations in my body

10 = Acknowledging anxiety and using it to provide insight into what is important

ANGER MANAGEMENT 1 2 3 4 5 6 7 8 9 10

1 = Having explosive outbursts, making threats, yelling, stuffing, devaluing, withholding, and other child-like dynamics when experiencing anger

10 = Consistently expressing anger in an adult-to-adult dynamic and externally processing anger via the use of therapeutic tools

DEPRESSION MANAGEMENT 1 2 3 4 5 6 7 8 9 10

1 = Choosing to engage in the victim orientation via avoiding emotional processing, not practicing self-care, and self-loathing every day for the past 7+ days

10 = Consistently choosing to use therapeutic tools, practice self-care, and take behavioral baby steps towards one's mission statement in life every day for the past 14 days

SHAME MANAGEMENT 1 2 3 4 5 6 7 8 9 10

1 = Believing I'm a bad person or a mistake (i.e. I'm a bad wife/I'm unlovable)

10 = Believing I'm a good person who made some mistakes

CO-DEPENDENCY 1 2 3 4 5 6 7 8 9 10

1 = Exhibiting rescuing behavior, failure to set boundaries, failure to implement consequences for boundary failures, and failing to process one's own issues during the past 7+ days.

10 = I have set/executed boundaries, taken behavioral baby steps towards my individual mission statement, acknowledged/processed my emotions, and living a life that is more internally than externally motivated

BOUNDARIES | 1 2 3 4 5 6 7 8 9 10

1 = A total lack of boundaries or the use of vague boundaries to justify withholding.

10 = Consistently maintaining boundaries and implementing consequences when boundaries are violated.

TRUST | 1 2 3 4 5 6 7 8 9 10

1 = Obsessing about your partner's recovery (OCD/co-dependency/anxiety), ignoring your partner's recovery work (denial/avoidance) and/or doubting your ability to make good decisions in the past 7+ days

10 = Consistently allowing your boundaries/consequences to work for you, expressing emotions in healthy transparent ways during FANOS check-ins and working towards building healthy attachment.

ACTING-IN | 1 2 3 4 5 6 7 8 9 10

1 = I withheld emotional/spiritual/physical intimacy in the past 7 days

10 = 6+ months of continuous emotional/spiritual/physical engagement

FORGIVENESS | 1 2 3 4 5 6 7 8 9 10

1 = Holding onto anger/resentment/bitterness and refusing to consider forgiveness

10 = I have fully processed my grief, accepted the betrayal, set boundaries, and reached a level of peace due to forgiveness

CONFLICT RESOLUTION | 1 2 3 4 5 6 7 8 9 10

1 = Displaying parent-to-child or child-to-child dynamics during conflict or avoiding conflict via people pleasing behaviors

10 = Consistently using healthy assertiveness and active listening with empathy to resolve conflict or reach a compromise in life every day for the past 14 days

SELF-WORTH | 1 2 3 4 5 6 7 8 9 10

1 = Feeling/believing I'm inadequate every day in the past 7+ days

10 = Feeling/believing I'm an adequate individual whose worth is not tied to another individual's behavior each day for the past 3+ months

SELF-CARE | 1 2 3 4 5 6 7 8 9 10

1 = Neglecting self-care behaviors/No self-care behaviors during the past 7+ days

10 = Consistently practicing self-care behaviors each day for the past year

Attachment wounds and parts within the Internal Family System. Human beings are created for healthy connection. From the way our eyes and bodies respond when communicating with others, to the way we feel when held in a warm embrace, behavioral evidence indicates that nurturing connection in relationships emotionally, chemically, and physically bond us together. However, trauma, addiction, neurodiversity, and developmental disruptions can alter how we emotionally, chemically, and physically attach due to safety issues.

In the previous section of reading, I briefly touched on the idea that psychological coping mechanisms, or parts of the self, can develop to protect one's wounded parts, such as the inner-child or inner-teenager. These parts can take the form of emotions, behavioral patterns, or ways of thinking in an effort to prevent or protect the wounded parts from experiencing the pain he or she once experienced in the past. In other words, these parts are trying to do their job of keeping your inner-child safe. However, sometimes their efforts are misguided or mal-adaptive, but it is important to not view them as bad because they are parts of you. Thus, part of the process of healing your own internal family system and building healthy attachment is identifying your various parts, understanding them, and working to allow your inner-adult to lead them in life.

Some protective or controlling parts I have noticed over the years doing partner recovery work are co-dependency, controller (acting-in), self-loather, self-saboteur, impression manager, compulsivity (acting-out), inner-teenager, idealizer/devaluer (critic/perfectionist), etc. It is important that you work through your anger, hatred, or fear associated with various parts so that they will be open to empathizing with your inner-adult and allow your healthy self to develop a healthy relationship with your wounded inner part(s).

At this point, you might be confused as to how your own internal family system (IFS) works. To help simplify the concept, let's explore the metaphor of an airplane with a pilot and passengers. Imagine for a moment, that all of your parts are on the airplane of life and flying towards the destination of your healthy self's vision for the future. Your healthy self, or inner-adult, is the intended pilot with the training and expertise to get you guys to your destination safely. However, due to each parts desire to protect the wounded part, occasionally, parts without the pilot's knowledge and expertise take control of the plane from time to time which deviates the plane from its' healthy flight plan. For example, when experiencing the pain of rejection, maybe your co-dependent part jumps into the cockpit and causes you to exhibit rescuing behavior to avoid or escape the pain of rejection once experienced by your wounded part. Or perhaps your anxiety surrounding your partner being mad at you causes you to shut down and withdraw when the controlling part takes control of the plane and causes you to avoid conflict. Those parts mean well, however, they simply lack the therapeutic tools and knowledge necessary to get the plane where it wants to go. Thus, part of partner's recovery work is learning who is flying your plane and why various triggers lead your plane to deviate from its' course due to the reactions of various protective and controlling parts.

The journey to cultivating healthy attachment amongst your internal family system requires patience, introspection, daily internal parts work, and therapeutic processing via individual therapy. In the coming exercises, we will work to identify your own parts and reflect on the origins of their development in your life.

EXERCISE 2-8: EXPLORING THE ORIGINS AND PRESENCE OF PARTS ACROSS YOUR LIFE (Part A)

Identifying various parts in addition to your inner-parent, inner-adult, and inner-child can be tricky. Rember, the protective and controlling parts exist to protect your inner-child and they don't always like their presence to be known because their goal is the self-preservation of your inner-child. Thus, getting access to your inner-child often requires going through the gatekeeping of your other parts. In this exercise, we will reflect on past experiences and graph the development and power of parts across your lifespan. Reflect back on **EXERCISE 2-5: CONNECTING TO YOUR INNER-CHILD** on pages 106-117 and **EXERCISE 2-6: CREATING A TRAUMA TIMELINE** on page 118. Consider all of the negative beliefs and painful emotions that surfaced during exercise 2-5 and when they occurred in exercise 2-6. As you reflect on those exercises, answer the following questions on the next page. If you have any questions on how to complete this exercise, consider walking through the exercise in an individual session with a therapist before your group.

What parts might have developed to deflect, protect, control, or propagate those beliefs and/or emotions? (i.e. co-dependency, controller (acting-in), self-loather, self-saboteur, impression manager, compulsivity (acting-out), inner-teenager, idealizer/devaluer (critic/perfectionist)

What parts tend to show up when those beliefs or emotions are triggered? (Make a list of each part and their corresponding belief)

How do those parts behaviorally manifest in your life? (i.e. controller may get angry and blame others, co-dependent might avoid setting boundaries, critic may shame yourself or others, etc.)

Do certain parts manifest when you experience certain somatic sensations? List the parts and associated sensations below. (i.e. rapid heart palpitations in the chest, heaviness in the shoulders, lump in the throat, discomfort in the gut, etc.).

EXERCISE 2-8: EXPLORING THE ORIGINS AND PRESENCE OF PARTS ACROSS YOUR LIFE (Part B)

Now that you have started to identify your various parts and their roles in protecting your inner-child from the pain of the past, it is time to explore the origins, power and prevalence of parts across your lifespan. On the line-graph timeline below, use various colors to mark the developmental origins of each part and chart the power (0 = no power, 10= high power) of each part across your lifespan to show fluctuations or consistency. You may want to reference your trauma timeline to assist in labeling origin points for each part.

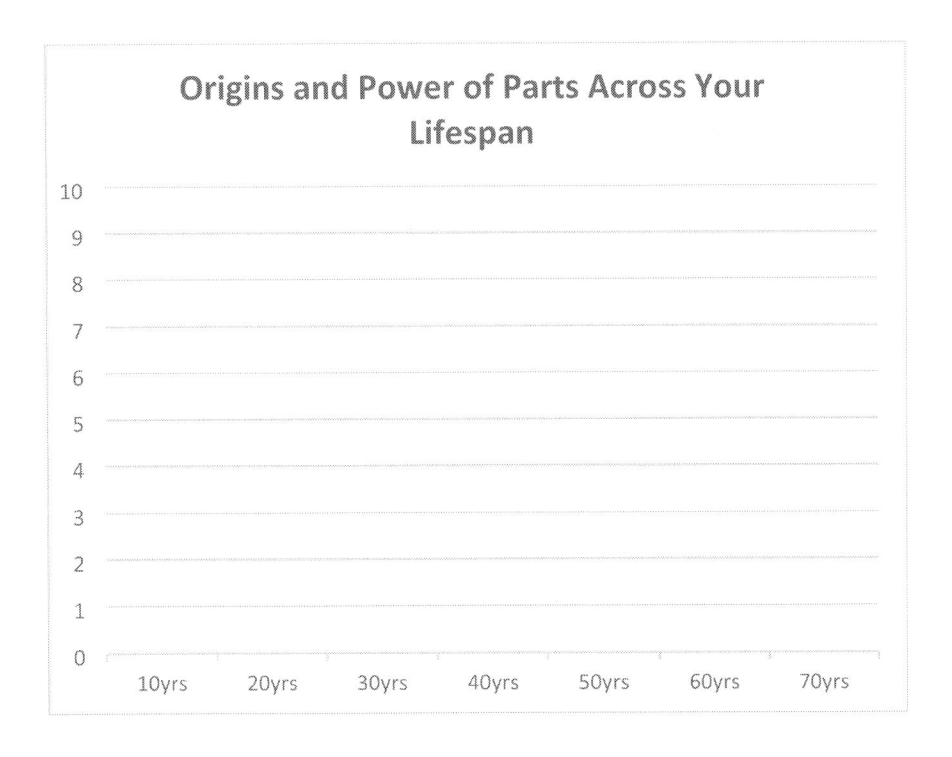

Origins and Power of Parts Across Your Lifespan

Power	10yrs	20yrs	30yrs	40yrs	50yrs	60yrs	70yrs
10							
9							
8							
7							
6							
5							
4							
3							
2							
1							
0							

EXERCISE 2-9: REFLECTION ON THE RELATIONSHIPS BETWEEN TRAUMATIC EXPERIENCES AND PARTS

Now that you have completed a trauma timeline and a parts timeline, it is important to explore the relationships between experiences and parts in the questions below.

When you look at your trauma timeline on pg. 118 and your parts timeline on pg. 137, what themes do you notice? _____

_____

_____

_____

_____

_____

_____

_____

_____

_____

How have your parts protected your inner-child from the pain of those experiences throughout your life? _____

How have your parts attempted to protect or control the pain associated with your partner's betrayal? _____

_____
_____
_____
_____
_____
_____

How have your parts shaped your perception of yourself? _____

_____
_____
_____
_____
_____
_____
_____

REMINDER: PARTS ARE NOT BAD! Parts are simply trying to protect or control/manage the pain of your inner-child. How can you work through any negative thoughts/emotions you may have towards your parts to empathize with their intentions and explore healthier action steps on your recovery journey? _____

_____

_____

_____

_____

_____

_____

_____

_____

_____

_____

_____

_____

_____

_____

Week 9

DATE	EXERCISES TO COMPLETE
	Read pages 142-150 and complete exercises: 2-10

OBJECTIVES

- Group processing of the letter to your parts.
- Exploring why trauma work is relevant before developing and implementing extensive boundaries and consequences in your life and relationship.

NOTES – INSIGHTS – THINGS TO EXPLORE IN THERAPY

ACCOUNTABILITY ISSUES – GOALS FOR THE WEEK

PARTNER RECOVERY GROWTH INDEX (PRGI)

DENIAL 1 2 3 4 5 6 7 8 9 10

1 = Believing my partner isn't an addict, denying my partner's progress, and/or denying the hurt and pain I am feeling because of my partner's addiction.

10 = Consistently feeling/expressing the pain caused by my partner's behavior and adjusting boundaries when appropriate due to therapeutic insight and progress.

ANXIETY MANAGEMENT 1 2 3 4 5 6 7 8 9 10

1 = Avoiding anxiety triggers and anxious feelings/sensations in my body

10 = Acknowledging anxiety and using it to provide insight into what is important

ANGER MANAGEMENT 1 2 3 4 5 6 7 8 9 10

1 = Having explosive outbursts, making threats, yelling, stuffing, devaluing, withholding, and other child-like dynamics when experiencing anger

10 = Consistently expressing anger in an adult-to-adult dynamic and externally processing anger via the use of therapeutic tools

DEPRESSION MANAGEMENT 1 2 3 4 5 6 7 8 9 10

1 = Choosing to engage in the victim orientation via avoiding emotional processing, not practicing self-care, and self-loathing every day for the past 7+ days

10 = Consistently choosing to use therapeutic tools, practice self-care, and take behavioral baby steps towards one's mission statement in life every day for the past 14 days

SHAME MANAGEMENT 1 2 3 4 5 6 7 8 9 10

1 = Believing I'm a bad person or a mistake (i.e. I'm a bad wife/I'm unlovable)

10 = Believing I'm a good person who made some mistakes

CO-DEPENDENCY 1 2 3 4 5 6 7 8 9 10

1 = Exhibiting rescuing behavior, failure to set boundaries, failure to implement consequences for boundary failures, and failing to process one's own issues during the past 7+ days.

10 = I have set/executed boundaries, taken behavioral baby steps towards my individual mission statement, acknowledged/processed my emotions, and living a life that is more internally than externally motivated

BOUNDARIES | 1 2 3 4 5 6 7 8 9 10

1 = A total lack of boundaries or the use of vague boundaries to justify withholding.

10 = Consistently maintaining boundaries and implementing consequences when boundaries are violated.

TRUST | 1 2 3 4 5 6 7 8 9 10

1 = Obsessing about your partner's recovery (OCD/co-dependency/anxiety), ignoring your partner's recovery work (denial/avoidance) and/or doubting your ability to make good decisions in the past 7+ days

10 = Consistently allowing your boundaries/consequences to work for you, expressing emotions in healthy transparent ways during FANOS check-ins and working towards building healthy attachment.

ACTING-IN | 1 2 3 4 5 6 7 8 9 10

1 = I withheld emotional/spiritual/physical intimacy in the past 7 days

10 = 6+ months of continuous emotional/spiritual/physical engagement

FORGIVENESS | 1 2 3 4 5 6 7 8 9 10

1 = Holding onto anger/resentment/bitterness and refusing to consider forgiveness

10 = I have fully processed my grief, accepted the betrayal, set boundaries, and reached a level of peace due to forgiveness

CONFLICT RESOLUTION | 1 2 3 4 5 6 7 8 9 10

1 = Displaying parent-to-child or child-to-child dynamics during conflict or avoiding conflict via people pleasing behaviors

10 = Consistently using healthy assertiveness and active listening with empathy to resolve conflict or reach a compromise in life every day for the past 14 days

SELF-WORTH | 1 2 3 4 5 6 7 8 9 10

1 = Feeling/believing I'm inadequate every day in the past 7+ days

10 = Feeling/believing I'm an adequate individual whose worth is not tied to another individual's behavior each day for the past 3+ months

SELF-CARE | 1 2 3 4 5 6 7 8 9 10

1 = Neglecting self-care behaviors/No self-care behaviors during the past 7+ days

10 = Consistently practicing self-care behaviors each day for the past year

It's all in the family... At this point of your recovery, you are likely discovering the role that external AND internal relationships have had in your life. Just like your trauma timeline tells an external story, your parts timeline tells an internal story. A lot of individuals who struggle with emotional dysregulation, emotional processing, and attachment are often disconnected and/or hyper-focused on limited aspects of their external and internal stories. In this chapter, we have been working on getting in touch with both stories so that you can connect with all aspects of yourself and process any pain that has been unprocessed in your life. As this pain manifests, the parts that have developed to protect or control your pain are likely attempting to go into overdrive to limit your inner-child from feeling the pain. This is normal because that is one of their roles in keeping you safe.

Now that you are gaining an awareness of the various names of your parts, it is not abnormal for individuals to view those parts as a "negative" aspect of the self. Ironically, this could not be further from the truth. Those parts exist and have existed for your survival. Thus, it is important to learn to empathize with them, understand them, and build a healthier relationship with them via empathy and boundaries. Therapeutic healing can occur when an individual recognizes the good intentions of their various parts, forgives the various parts for any pain and suffering that has occurred due to their roles in one's life, and moves forward in life by allowing the healthy inner adult to "fly the plane" by setting healthy boundaries with the other parts. This is easier said than done because a lot of your protective and controlling parts have been "flying the plane" when triggered for a significant period of time in your life.

The dance between the parts of your internal family system is fluid and requires developing internal attunement and taking a nonjudgemental stance towards parts when you are triggered. Daily parts work and intentionality about being mindfully present with yourself can go a long way towards helping your internal family system heal. Talk with your therapist or life coach about ways in which you can take action steps to develop or maintain a healthier internal family system.

EXERCISE 2-10: EMOTIONALLY CONNECTING WITH YOUR INTERNAL PARTS

In this exercise, you will write a letter to all of your identified parts. In the letter, you will thank them (be specific and refer to them by name) for the ways in which they have kept you safe in your life. Also communicate empathy towards each part for the love behind their intentions. Finally, communicate healthy boundaries and action steps you are going to take moving forward with them so that you can begin to "fly the plane" and get all of your parts moving towards a healthy vision in your life. Close the letter by acknowledging your emotions and why it is important for things to change.

Dear (List all of your parts by name):

_____

_____

_____

_____

With all my love moving forward,

Next steps ... Processing trauma takes time. While we have extensively taken a look at your trauma and the psychological adaptations that have developed to cope with those experiences, it still takes time, individual therapy, and practicing new healthy coping behaviors to establish new neuropathways of recovery growth. It is important to have grace with yourself and ask for grace from others as you work through your pain and regain confidence, trust, and self-worth that were impacted by your experiences before and after your partner came into your life. As stated in the opening of this text, the purpose in addressing those experiences was to assist you in stabilizing your behavioral/emotion-minded responses to the trauma of learning your partner was an addict. While this process has not yet addressed all of your grief and pain (we will do this in future chapters), it has hopefully allowed you to recognize the importance of your inner-adult making wise-minded decisions about your current circumstances inside and outside of your relationship. Perhaps the greatest decision you will make, will be to create and implement boundaries for internally healing from the betrayal. This allows healthy action steps concerning the potential restoration of trust in your relationship. Let's explore that in the next chapter!

Week 10

DATE	EXERCISES TO COMPLETE
	Read pages 151-162 and complete exercises: 3-1 and 3-2

OBJECTIVES

- Exploring the role of boundaries in relationships.
- Group processing of behavorial boundaries exercises and why such boundaries are important when you have experienced sexual and/or emotional betrayal.

NOTES – INSIGHTS – THINGS TO EXPLORE IN THERAPY

ACCOUNTABILITY ISSUES – GOALS FOR THE WEEK

PARTNER RECOVERY GROWTH INDEX (PRGI)

DENIAL 1 2 3 4 5 6 7 8 9 10

1 = Believing my partner isn't an addict, denying my partner's progress, and/or denying the hurt and pain I am feeling because of my partner's addiction.

10 = Consistently feeling/expressing the pain caused by my partner's behavior and adjusting boundaries when appropriate due to therapeutic insight and progress.

ANXIETY MANAGEMENT 1 2 3 4 5 6 7 8 9 10

1 = Avoiding anxiety triggers and anxious feelings/sensations in my body

10 = Acknowledging anxiety and using it to provide insight into what is important

ANGER MANAGEMENT 1 2 3 4 5 6 7 8 9 10

1 = Having explosive outbursts, making threats, yelling, stuffing, devaluing, withholding, and other child-like dynamics when experiencing anger

10 = Consistently expressing anger in an adult-to-adult dynamic and externally processing anger via the use of therapeutic tools

DEPRESSION MANAGEMENT 1 2 3 4 5 6 7 8 9 10

1 = Choosing to engage in the victim orientation via avoiding emotional processing, not practicing self-care, and self-loathing every day for the past 7+ days

10 = Consistently choosing to use therapeutic tools, practice self-care, and take behavioral baby steps towards one's mission statement in life every day for the past 14 days

SHAME MANAGEMENT 1 2 3 4 5 6 7 8 9 10

1 = Believing I'm a bad person or a mistake (i.e. I'm a bad wife/I'm unlovable)

10 = Believing I'm a good person who made some mistakes

CO-DEPENDENCY 1 2 3 4 5 6 7 8 9 10

1 = Exhibiting rescuing behavior, failure to set boundaries, failure to implement consequences for boundary failures, and failing to process one's own issues during the past 7+ days.

10 = I have set/executed boundaries, taken behavioral baby steps towards my individual mission statement, acknowledged/processed my emotions, and living a life that is more internally than externally motivated

BOUNDARIES | 1 2 3 4 5 6 7 8 9 10

1 = A total lack of boundaries or the use of vague boundaries to justify withholding.

10 = Consistently maintaining boundaries and implementing consequences when boundaries are violated.

TRUST | 1 2 3 4 5 6 7 8 9 10

1 = Obsessing about your partner's recovery (OCD/co-dependency/anxiety), ignoring your partner's recovery work (denial/avoidance) and/or doubting your ability to make good decisions in the past 7+ days

10 = Consistently allowing your boundaries/consequences to work for you, expressing emotions in healthy transparent ways during FANOS check-ins and working towards building healthy attachment.

ACTING-IN | 1 2 3 4 5 6 7 8 9 10

1 = I withheld emotional/spiritual/physical intimacy in the past 7 days

10 = 6+ months of continuous emotional/spiritual/physical engagement

FORGIVENESS | 1 2 3 4 5 6 7 8 9 10

1 = Holding onto anger/resentment/bitterness and refusing to consider forgiveness

10 = I have fully processed my grief, accepted the betrayal, set boundaries, and reached a level of peace due to forgiveness

CONFLICT RESOLUTION | 1 2 3 4 5 6 7 8 9 10

1 = Displaying parent-to-child or child-to-child dynamics during conflict or avoiding conflict via people pleasing behaviors

10 = Consistently using healthy assertiveness and active listening with empathy to resolve conflict or reach a compromise in life every day for the past 14 days

SELF-WORTH | 1 2 3 4 5 6 7 8 9 10

1 = Feeling/believing I'm inadequate every day in the past 7+ days

10 = Feeling/believing I'm an adequate individual whose worth is not tied to another individual's behavior each day for the past 3+ months

SELF-CARE | 1 2 3 4 5 6 7 8 9 10

1 = Neglecting self-care behaviors/No self-care behaviors during the past 7+ days

10 = Consistently practicing self-care behaviors each day for the past year

Chapter 3: The Importance of Boundaries in Healing from Trauma

What are boundaries and why are they so important in a relationship? Boundaries are fixed limits on behaviors or emotions that keep you safe physically, emotionally, and mentally. Oftentimes couples do not even think about their need for boundaries until it is too late. To make matters worse, a sex addict can blow past boundaries that are spoken, unspoken, and lacking in consequences. In fact, the trauma you have begun to process in chapter 2 is a product of your partner breaking the boundaries that seemed to be common sense in the relationship. If trust is to be rebuilt, new boundaries get to be set. Boundaries that come with consequences.

We have recently identified various parts that may play a role in your ability to effectively develop, implement and enforce boundaries. It is imperative to do daily parts work to continue the process of identifying the presence of parts and not allow other parts, such as co-dependency, to control your boundaries and consequences.

The first issue to address with boundaries are the various categories in which damaging and or triggering behavior can occur. Consider the following categories:

Technology: Phones, computers, tablets, and gaming systems typically are a challenge for individuals struggling with acting out/acting in behavior such as porn, chatting, cruising, sexting, and having an emotional affair. Sometimes boundaries regarding access, accountability, and transparency are necessary with technology while an individual is working on establishing sobriety.

Communication: Since sexual acting out/acting in is an intimacy disorder, setting boundaries for communication in the relationship is pivotal to creating emotional safety. Lying, gaslighting, angry outbursts, avoiding emotional conversation, and avoiding eye contact are many communication boundaries that can be addressed in your relationship. You can also consider establishing a daily/weekly check-in communication exercise to highlight all of the aforementioned concerns.

Therapeutic: Therapeutic boundaries are all about ensuring that your partner is working his or her recovery. Attending individual therapy, attending a clinician-led therapy group, and attending a 12-step meeting are therapeutic boundaries you get to set. If your partner is unwilling to work on his or her recovery, what does that say about how he or she values the pain you are experiencing regarding his or her acting out behavior?

People and Places: If your partner has known acting out partners, it is okay for you to request that they cut off all communication with the individual(s). If your partner has a history of attending certain establishments (strip clubs/bars/adult stores/hotels/certain cities, etc.) it is okay for you to establish boundaries with your partner not visiting those establishments. If you partner must work with an individual or stay at a particular hotel due to work, it is okay for you to voice your concerns about how that hurts you and decide if that is a negotiable or non-negotiable boundary.

Sexual: In the early stages of recovery, partners of sex addicts often feel an anxious pressure surrounding the need to be physically intimate with his or her partner so she or he doesn't act out again. THIS IS YOUR TRAUMA BRAIN TALKING. You get to say no to sexual behavior if it is triggering, demeaning, object-related, or anger-inducing.

EXERCISE 3-1: REFLECTING ON MY MOTIVATION FOR PHYSICAL INTIMACY

The best way to determine if your desire for physical intimacy with your partner is healthy, is to reflect on your motivation. Ask yourself the following questions:

1. *Am I anxious and looking to calm my nerves?*

2. *Am I scared and wanting to prevent him or her from acting out?*

3. *Am I feeling insecure and wanting him or her to validate my worth sexually?*

4. *Am I sad and needing to numb my pain sexually?*

5. *Am I feeling sorry for him or her and wanting to make him or her feel better?*

6. *Am I afraid of being abandoned/alone?*

7. *Am I feeling like I need to sexually reward him or her for working on his or her recovery?*

8.   *Am I angry and wanting to numb my anger sexually and/or take out my frustration sexually on my partner?*

If the answer to any of these questions is a yes, that likely indicates an object-related need for sex. Object-related sex is when an individual engages in sexual behavior for his or her own gratification or the gratification of his or her partner without relational connection. Healthy Attachment (HA) sex is grounded in eye contact, emotionally engaging conversation/validation, and a true desire for the sexual experience to be connecting. The likelihood that you have been in a predominantly object-related relationship with your partner due to his or her addiction is high. We know this is painful to accept, but that is why it is important to reflect on developing healthy sexual boundaries in your relationship.

What emotions surface when you reflect on the unhealthy motivations for physical intimacy in your relationship?

_____

_____

_____

EXERCISE 3-2: REFLECTING ON MY EMOTIONAL, PHYSICAL, AND SAFETY NEEDS RELATED TO PHYSICAL INTIMACY

Reflect on the current aspects of sexuality in your relationship to potentially address via boundaries by answering the following questions. Make sure to provide your rational in the space provided.

1. Am I comfortable with my partner seeing me naked? _____

   _____

   _____

2. Am I comfortable with being sexually intimate with my partner? _____

   _____

   _____

3. If I am comfortable with being sexually intimate, am I comfortable with my partner initiating sexual behavior or do I need that control to feel emotionally safe? _____

4. *Am I comfortable with certain sexual behaviors, positions, locations that I now recognize as potentially triggering to me?*

5. *Am I comfortable with the lack of my partner initiating physical intimacy?*

6. *Am I comfortable with digital sexual behavior in our relationship?* _____

_____

_____

_____

Review your response to question 4 in Exercise 2-4 of chapter 2 and your work in Exercises 3-1 and 3-2. What are your physical, emotional, and mental boundary needs? Make short-hand notes here for reflection when developing your boundaries in Exercise 3-3.

_____

_____

_____

_____

_____

_____

_____

_____

_____

Week 11

DATE	EXERCISES TO COMPLETE
	Read pages 163-199 and complete exercises: 3-3 and 3-4

OBJECTIVES

- Developing various boundaries and consequences.
- Exploring how to communicate boundaries and consequences to your partner.

NOTES – INSIGHTS – THINGS TO EXPLORE IN THERAPY

_____
_____
_____
_____
_____
_____
_____
_____
_____
_____

ACCOUNTABILITY ISSUES – GOALS FOR THE WEEK

_____
_____
_____
_____
_____
_____
_____
_____
_____
_____
_____

PARTNER RECOVERY GROWTH INDEX (PRGI)

DENIAL 1 2 3 4 5 6 7 8 9 10

1 = Believing my partner isn't an addict, denying my partner's progress, and/or denying the hurt and pain I am feeling because of my partner's addiction.

10 = Consistently feeling/expressing the pain caused by my partner's behavior and adjusting boundaries when appropriate due to therapeutic insight and progress.

ANXIETY MANAGEMENT 1 2 3 4 5 6 7 8 9 10

1 = Avoiding anxiety triggers and anxious feelings/sensations in my body

10 = Acknowledging anxiety and using it to provide insight into what is important

ANGER MANAGEMENT 1 2 3 4 5 6 7 8 9 10

1 = Having explosive outbursts, making threats, yelling, stuffing, devaluing, withholding, and other child-like dynamics when experiencing anger

10 = Consistently expressing anger in an adult-to-adult dynamic and externally processing anger via the use of therapeutic tools

DEPRESSION MANAGEMENT 1 2 3 4 5 6 7 8 9 10

1 = Choosing to engage in the victim orientation via avoiding emotional processing, not practicing self-care, and self-loathing every day for the past 7+ days

10 = Consistently choosing to use therapeutic tools, practice self-care, and take behavioral baby steps towards one's mission statement in life every day for the past 14 days

SHAME MANAGEMENT 1 2 3 4 5 6 7 8 9 10

1 = Believing I'm a bad person or a mistake (i.e. I'm a bad wife/I'm unlovable)

10 = Believing I'm a good person who made some mistakes

CO-DEPENDENCY 1 2 3 4 5 6 7 8 9 10

1 = Exhibiting rescuing behavior, failure to set boundaries, failure to implement consequences for boundary failures, and failing to process one's own issues during the past 7+ days.

10 = I have set/executed boundaries, taken behavioral baby steps towards my individual mission statement, acknowledged/processed my emotions, and living a life that is more internally than externally motivated

BOUNDARIES | 1 2 3 4 5 6 7 8 9 10

1 = A total lack of boundaries or the use of vague boundaries to justify withholding.

10 = Consistently maintaining boundaries and implementing consequences when boundaries are violated.

TRUST | 1 2 3 4 5 6 7 8 9 10

1 = Obsessing about your partner's recovery (OCD/co-dependency/anxiety), ignoring your partner's recovery work (denial/avoidance) and/or doubting your ability to make good decisions in the past 7+ days

10 = Consistently allowing your boundaries/consequences to work for you, expressing emotions in healthy transparent ways during FANOS check-ins and working towards building healthy attachment.

ACTING-IN | 1 2 3 4 5 6 7 8 9 10

1 = I withheld emotional/spiritual/physical intimacy in the past 7 days

10 = 6+ months of continuous emotional/spiritual/physical engagement

FORGIVENESS | 1 2 3 4 5 6 7 8 9 10

1 = Holding onto anger/resentment/bitterness and refusing to consider forgiveness

10 = I have fully processed my grief, accepted the betrayal, set boundaries, and reached a level of peace due to forgiveness

CONFLICT RESOLUTION | 1 2 3 4 5 6 7 8 9 10

1 = Displaying parent-to-child or child-to-child dynamics during conflict or avoiding conflict via people pleasing behaviors

10 = Consistently using healthy assertiveness and active listening with empathy to resolve conflict or reach a compromise in life every day for the past 14 days

SELF-WORTH | 1 2 3 4 5 6 7 8 9 10

1 = Feeling/believing I'm inadequate every day in the past 7+ days

10 = Feeling/believing I'm an adequate individual whose worth is not tied to another individual's behavior each day for the past 3+ months

SELF-CARE | 1 2 3 4 5 6 7 8 9 10

1 = Neglecting self-care behaviors/No self-care behaviors during the past 7+ days

10 = Consistently practicing self-care behaviors each day for the past year

A non-negotiable boundary is a boundary that you are unwilling to compromise on at any time. A negotiated boundary is a boundary that you are willing to negotiate on later in time after trust has been restored. In the following examples you will see both non-negotiable and negotiable boundaries.

Example: If you have another affair the following consequences are on the table: Divorce, Legal Separation, Physical Separation, etc.

Example: If you relapse and look at porn the following consequences are on the table: Divorce, Separation, Sleeping on the couch for a week, etc.

Example: If you allow another female to ride alone with you in the car the following consequences are on the table: Sleeping on the couch for 3 days or you will have to have a male co-worker drive you to and from work for a week.

Example: I expect you to initiate emotional intimacy 5 out of 7 days. If this is not met, you will have massage my feet for 15 minutes while telling me about your emotions from the past day.

Example: For the foreseeable future, you will have to send me pictures of where you are at. This will help to rebuild my trust that you are where you say you are at.

Example: For the foreseeable, you will have to call me when you leave work to let me know you are on your way home/answer the phone every time I call you.

The following pages are designed for you to process the boundaries you get to set and why you are setting them. Please take your time and think about the different categories of physical, emotional, and mental boundaries you get to set with your partner. You may also want to consider a tiered system of consequences for multiple offenses. If your partner looks at porn again, do you really want to implement a no-tolerance policy of divorce, or do you make the first offense therapeutic separation for 1-2 weeks, second offense therapeutic separation for 3 months, third offense therapeutic separation for 6 months, fourth offense divorce, etc.? The key to answering this question is your ability to follow through with the consequences. If you set a consequence but struggle to see it through, your partner will likely exploit your avoidance and you will end up getting hurt. The extra space provided at the end of each boundary you make can be used for additional notes you may want to add as you and your therapist discuss each boundary.

Exercise 3-3: Boundary Development Worksheets

Boundary # 1

_____

_____

_____

Is this boundary negotiable or non-negotiable? Why?

_____

_____

What is the consequence(s) if this boundary is broken?

_____

_____

What is the rationale behind this boundary?

_____

_____

How does this boundary protect you physically?

_____

_____

How does this boundary protect you emotionally?

How does this boundary create safety in your relationship while you are working your recovery?

What internal parts might make the implementation of this boundary difficult in your relationship?

What behavioral consequence will you implement for yourself if you fail to stick to this boundary and consequence?

Boundary # 2

_____

_____

_____

Is this boundary negotiable or non-negotiable? Why?

_____

_____

What is the consequence(s) if this boundary is broken?

_____

_____

What is the rationale behind this boundary?

_____

_____

How does this boundary protect you physically?

_____

_____

How does this boundary protect you emotionally?

How does this boundary create safety in your relationship while you are working your recovery?

What internal parts might make the implementation of this boundary difficult in your relationship?

What behavioral consequence will you implement for yourself if you fail to stick to this boundary and consequence?

Boundary # 3

_____

_____

_____

Is this boundary negotiable or non-negotiable? Why?

_____

_____

What is the consequence(s) if this boundary is broken?

_____

_____

What is the rationale behind this boundary?

_____

_____

How does this boundary protect you physically?

_____

_____

How does this boundary protect you emotionally?

_____

_____

How does this boundary create safety in your relationship while you are working your recovery?

_____

_____

What internal parts might make the implementation of this boundary difficult in your relationship?

_____

_____

What behavioral consequence will you implement for yourself if you fail to stick to this boundary and consequence?

_____

_____

_____

_____

Boundary # 4

_____

_____

_____

Is this boundary negotiable or non-negotiable? Why?

_____

_____

What is the consequence(s) if this boundary is broken?

_____

_____

What is the rationale behind this boundary?

_____

_____

How does this boundary protect you physically?

_____

_____

How does this boundary protect you emotionally?

How does this boundary create safety in your relationship while you are working your recovery?

What internal parts might make the implementation of this boundary difficult in your relationship?

What behavioral consequence will you implement for yourself if you fail to stick to this boundary and consequence?

Boundary # 5

_____

_____

_____

Is this boundary negotiable or non-negotiable? Why?

_____

_____

What is the consequence(s) if this boundary is broken?

_____

_____

What is the rationale behind this boundary?

_____

_____

How does this boundary protect you physically?

_____

_____

How does this boundary protect you emotionally?

_____

_____

How does this boundary create safety in your relationship while you are working your recovery?

_____

_____

What internal parts might make the implementation of this boundary difficult in your relationship?

_____

_____

What behavioral consequence will you implement for yourself if you fail to stick to this boundary and consequence?

_____

_____

_____

Boundary # 6

_____

_____

_____

Is this boundary negotiable or non-negotiable? Why?

_____

_____

What is the consequence(s) if this boundary is broken?

_____

_____

What is the rationale behind this boundary?

_____

_____

How does this boundary protect you physically?

_____

_____

How does this boundary protect you emotionally?

_____

_____

How does this boundary create safety in your relationship while you are working your recovery?

_____

_____

What internal parts might make the implementation of this boundary difficult in your relationship?

_____

_____

What behavioral consequence will you implement for yourself if you fail to stick to this boundary and consequence?

_____

_____

_____

Boundary # 7

_____

_____

_____

Is this boundary negotiable or non-negotiable? Why?

_____

_____

What is the consequence(s) if this boundary is broken?

_____

_____

What is the rationale behind this boundary?

_____

_____

How does this boundary protect you physically?

_____

_____

How does this boundary protect you emotionally?

_____

_____

How does this boundary create safety in your relationship while you are working your recovery?

_____

_____

What internal parts might make the implementation of this boundary difficult in your relationship?

_____

_____

What behavioral consequence will you implement for yourself if you fail to stick to this boundary and consequence?

_____

_____

_____

_____

Boundary # 8

_____

_____

_____

Is this boundary negotiable or non-negotiable? Why?

_____

_____

What is the consequence(s) if this boundary is broken?

_____

_____

What is the rationale behind this boundary?

_____

_____

How does this boundary protect you physically?

_____

_____

How does this boundary protect you emotionally?

How does this boundary create safety in your relationship while you are working your recovery?

What internal parts might make the implementation of this boundary difficult in your relationship?

What behavioral consequence will you implement for yourself if you fail to stick to this boundary and consequence?

Boundary # 9

_____

_____

_____

Is this boundary negotiable or non-negotiable? Why?

_____

_____

What is the consequence(s) if this boundary is broken?

_____

_____

What is the rationale behind this boundary?

_____

_____

How does this boundary protect you physically?

_____

_____

How does this boundary protect you emotionally?

_____

_____

How does this boundary create safety in your relationship while you are working your recovery?

_____

_____

What internal parts might make the implementation of this boundary difficult in your relationship?

_____

_____

What behavioral consequence will you implement for yourself if you fail to stick to this boundary and consequence?

_____

_____

_____

_____

Boundary # 10

_____
_____
_____

Is this boundary negotiable or non-negotiable? Why?

_____
_____

What is the consequence(s) if this boundary is broken?

_____
_____

What is the rationale behind this boundary?

_____
_____

How does this boundary protect you physically?

_____
_____

How does this boundary protect you emotionally?

How does this boundary create safety in your relationship while you are working your recovery?

What internal parts might make the implementation of this boundary difficult in your relationship?

What behavioral consequence will you implement for yourself if you fail to stick to this boundary and consequence?

Boundary # 11

_____

_____

_____

Is this boundary negotiable or non-negotiable? Why?

_____

_____

What is the consequence(s) if this boundary is broken?

_____

_____

What is the rationale behind this boundary?

_____

_____

How does this boundary protect you physically?

_____

_____

How does this boundary protect you emotionally?

How does this boundary create safety in your relationship while you are working your recovery?

What internal parts might make the implementation of this boundary difficult in your relationship?

What behavioral consequence will you implement for yourself if you fail to stick to this boundary and consequence?

Boundary # 12

_____

_____

_____

Is this boundary negotiable or non-negotiable? Why?

_____

_____

What is the consequence(s) if this boundary is broken?

_____

_____

What is the rationale behind this boundary?

_____

_____

How does this boundary protect you physically?

_____

_____

How does this boundary protect you emotionally?

_____

_____

How does this boundary create safety in your relationship while you are working your recovery?

_____

_____

What internal parts might make the implementation of this boundary difficult in your relationship?

_____

_____

What behavioral consequence will you implement for yourself if you fail to stick to this boundary and consequence?

_____

_____

_____

Boundary # 13

_____

_____

_____

Is this boundary negotiable or non-negotiable? Why?

_____

_____

What is the consequence(s) if this boundary is broken?

_____

_____

What is the rationale behind this boundary?

_____

_____

How does this boundary protect you physically?

_____

_____

How does this boundary protect you emotionally?

_____

_____

How does this boundary create safety in your relationship while you are working your recovery?

_____

_____

What internal parts might make the implementation of this boundary difficult in your relationship?

_____

_____

What behavioral consequence will you implement for yourself if you fail to stick to this boundary and consequence?

_____

_____

_____

_____

Boundary # 14

_____

_____
_____

Is this boundary negotiable or non-negotiable? Why?

_____
_____

What is the consequence(s) if this boundary is broken?

_____
_____

What is the rationale behind this boundary?

_____
_____

How does this boundary protect you physically?

_____
_____

How does this boundary protect you emotionally?

How does this boundary create safety in your relationship while you are working your recovery?

What internal parts might make the implementation of this boundary difficult in your relationship?

What behavioral consequence will you implement for yourself if you fail to stick to this boundary and consequence?

Boundary # 15

_____

_____

_____

Is this boundary negotiable or non-negotiable? Why?

_____

_____

What is the consequence(s) if this boundary is broken?

_____

_____

What is the rationale behind this boundary?

_____

_____

How does this boundary protect you physically?

_____

_____

How does this boundary protect you emotionally?

_____

_____

How does this boundary create safety in your relationship while you are working your recovery?

_____

_____

What internal parts might make the implementation of this boundary difficult in your relationship?

_____

_____

What behavioral consequence will you implement for yourself if you fail to stick to this boundary and consequence?

_____

_____

_____

EXERCISE 3-4: TELLING YOUR BOUNDARIES AND CONSEQUENCES TO YOUR PARTNER

Once you have completed developing and processing your boundaries and consequences with your therapist, it is time to decide how you will tell your partner. This can happen with 2 possible options.

Option 1: You and your partner attend a joint session where you can read your boundaries and consequences to your partner with the support of your therapist. This option will also allow the therapist to challenge your partner if he or she is resistant to the implementation of the boundaries.

Option 2: You will read your boundaries and consequences to your partner in a private location where you can dialogue about the implementation of the boundaries without interruption from children, work, or friends.

I commit to disclosing my boundaries and consequences to my partner on _____ . I will have _____

_____ assist in holding me accountable.

Week 12

DATE	EXERCISES TO COMPLETE
	Read pages 200-216 and complete exercises: 4-1, 4-2 and 4-3

OBJECTIVES

- Exploring the process of grief after partner betrayal.
- Group processing of the consequences of your partner's acting out/acting in behavior in your life.

NOTES – INSIGHTS – THINGS TO EXPLORE IN THERAPY

ACCOUNTABILITY ISSUES – GOALS FOR THE WEEK

PARTNER RECOVERY GROWTH INDEX (PRGI)

DENIAL 1 2 3 4 5 6 7 8 9 10

1 = Believing my partner isn't an addict, denying my partner's progress, and/or denying the hurt and pain I am feeling because of my partner's addiction.

10 = Consistently feeling/expressing the pain caused by my partner's behavior and adjusting boundaries when appropriate due to therapeutic insight and progress.

ANXIETY MANAGEMENT 1 2 3 4 5 6 7 8 9 10

1 = Avoiding anxiety triggers and anxious feelings/sensations in my body

10 = Acknowledging anxiety and using it to provide insight into what is important

ANGER MANAGEMENT 1 2 3 4 5 6 7 8 9 10

1 = Having explosive outbursts, making threats, yelling, stuffing, devaluing, withholding, and other child-like dynamics when experiencing anger

10 = Consistently expressing anger in an adult-to-adult dynamic and externally processing anger via the use of therapeutic tools

DEPRESSION MANAGEMENT 1 2 3 4 5 6 7 8 9 10

1 = Choosing to engage in the victim orientation via avoiding emotional processing, not practicing self-care, and self-loathing every day for the past 7+ days

10 = Consistently choosing to use therapeutic tools, practice self-care, and take behavioral baby steps towards one's mission statement in life every day for the past 14 days

SHAME MANAGEMENT 1 2 3 4 5 6 7 8 9 10

1 = Believing I'm a bad person or a mistake (i.e. I'm a bad wife/I'm unlovable)

10 = Believing I'm a good person who made some mistakes

CO-DEPENDENCY 1 2 3 4 5 6 7 8 9 10

1 = Exhibiting rescuing behavior, failure to set boundaries, failure to implement consequences for boundary failures, and failing to process one's own issues during the past 7+ days.

10 = I have set/executed boundaries, taken behavioral baby steps towards my individual mission statement, acknowledged/processed my emotions, and living a life that is more internally than externally motivated

BOUNDARIES | 1 2 3 4 5 6 7 8 9 10

1 = A total lack of boundaries or the use of vague boundaries to justify withholding.

10 = Consistently maintaining boundaries and implementing consequences when boundaries are violated.

TRUST | 1 2 3 4 5 6 7 8 9 10

1 = Obsessing about your partner's recovery (OCD/co-dependency/anxiety), ignoring your partner's recovery work (denial/avoidance) and/or doubting your ability to make good decisions in the past 7+ days

10 = Consistently allowing your boundaries/consequences to work for you, expressing emotions in healthy transparent ways during FANOS check-ins and working towards building healthy attachment.

ACTING-IN | 1 2 3 4 5 6 7 8 9 10

1 = I withheld emotional/spiritual/physical intimacy in the past 7 days

10 = 6+ months of continuous emotional/spiritual/physical engagement

FORGIVENESS | 1 2 3 4 5 6 7 8 9 10

1 = Holding onto anger/resentment/bitterness and refusing to consider forgiveness

10 = I have fully processed my grief, accepted the betrayal, set boundaries, and reached a level of peace due to forgiveness

CONFLICT RESOLUTION | 1 2 3 4 5 6 7 8 9 10

1 = Displaying parent-to-child or child-to-child dynamics during conflict or avoiding conflict via people pleasing behaviors

10 = Consistently using healthy assertiveness and active listening with empathy to resolve conflict or reach a compromise in life every day for the past 14 days

SELF-WORTH | 1 2 3 4 5 6 7 8 9 10

1 = Feeling/believing I'm inadequate every day in the past 7+ days

10 = Feeling/believing I'm an adequate individual whose worth is not tied to another individual's behavior each day for the past 3+ months

SELF-CARE | 1 2 3 4 5 6 7 8 9 10

1 = Neglecting self-care behaviors/No self-care behaviors during the past 7+ days

10 = Consistently practicing self-care behaviors each day for the past year

Chapter 4: Navigating the Maze of Grief

During my practicum in graduate school, I worked at a grief and loss center that specialized in individual and group treatment for processing grief and unexpected loss. In the field of clinical mental health counseling, grief is a specialization that some clinicians avoid because there is no quick fix to assisting a client walking through the worst pain a human being can experience. During my tenure at the center, I quickly realized the individual nature of grief. In the clinician-led support group at the center, some people had been stuck in the grief process for a decade. Others were less than a year into a loss but making tremendous strides in their grief process. My supervisor was quick to point out that there wasn't a specific structure to grief, despite the clinical 5 stages of denial, anger, sadness, bargaining, and acceptance. Everyone grieves at his or her own pace. Grieving well is pushing yourself to do the work of grieving at a pace that is necessary for you. Trouble comes when we spend too much time in denial to avoid the pain associated with the loss. Sometimes, we vacillate between various stages due to sensory stimuli triggers, pain, or simply not wanting to give up the idea that things will never be the same due to the unexpected loss. For the partner of someone who struggles with acting out/acting in, the reality is that the addict is NOT the person he or she claimed to be. This reality feels like a death, in the sense that the person you loved, cherished, and believed to be faithful was not the person you thought he or she was. In reality, he or she turned out to be a deceitful liar who betrayed you in an intimate way. Accepting that when you love someone with whom you have built a life is a painful type of grief that requires time to process. Sometimes, the reality cannot be accepted, and the partner realizes that the relationship cannot be saved. However, it is impossible to make this decision in wise mind if the partner hasn't fully processed his or her trauma triggers and grieved the losses associated with the betrayal. The work in this chapter is designed to assist you in progressing through your individual grief maze associated with your betrayal. You likely will not have completed your grief by the end of this chapter, but you will have tapped into your emotions associated with various stages within the grief process.

EXERCISE 4-1: IMPACT INVENTORY

Make a list of the individual impacts your partner's acting out/acting in behavior has had in your life. Make sure that you list all 40.

Examples: "I had to have an STD screening test."

"I feel insecure with my physical appearance."

1._____

2._____

3._____

4._____

5._____

6._____

7._____

8._____

9._____

10._____

11._____

12._____

13._____

14._____

15._____

16._____

17._____

18._____

19._____

20._____

21._____

22._____

23._____

24._____

25._____

26. _____
27. _____
28. _____
29. _____
30. _____
31. _____
32. _____
33. _____
34. _____
35. _____
36. _____
37. _____
38. _____
39. _____
40. _____

EXERCISE 4-2: REFLECTION ON THE IMPACT INVENTORY

Now that you have completed your impact inventory, answer the following questions:

1. What emotions came up while completing your impact inventory?

_____

_____

_____

_____

2. What was the most difficult part of completing the impact inventory?

_____

_____

_____

_____

_____

3. What items on the impact inventory do you avoid thinking about and talking about with others?

4. How can the group help you cope with the pain of your grief?

5. Where do you think you were in terms of denial before completing the impact inventory?

EXERCISE 4-3: LIST OF RATIONALIZATIONS

Rationalizing, or using reasoning to explain things that are questionable is a product of denial/avoidance. In this exercise, list various things that you noticed about your partner that you rationalized to avoid emotional distress/pain.

Example: "He is just working late."

> "He is a good provider, so he deserves hours alone in the study with the door closed."

> "He is just daydreaming. There is no way he would stare at a female in public right in front of me and the kids."

> "He just has a high sex-drive and I don't, so it is okay for him to look at porn."

> "He is just tired. It is okay for him to not respond to my sexual advances."

> "I'm just being paranoid. He has a right to get upset when I tell him I sense a disconnection in our relationship."

1. _____

Emotions now when thinking about this rationalization:

_____

_____

2. _____

Emotions now when thinking about this rationalization:

_____

_____

3. _____

Emotions now when thinking about this rationalization:

_____

_____

4. _____

Emotions now when thinking about this rationalization:

_____

_____

5. _____

Emotions now when thinking about this rationalization:

_____

_____

6. _____

Emotions now when thinking about this rationalization:

_____

_____

7. _____

Emotions now when thinking about this rationalization:

_____

_____

8. _____

Emotions now when thinking about this rationalization:

_____

_____

9. _____

Emotions now when thinking about this rationalization:

_____

_____

10. _____

Emotions now when thinking about this rationalization:

_____

_____

How have these rationalizations impacted your perception of yourself? What emotions surface when making those connections?

_____

_____

_____

_____

_____

_____

_____

_____

Week 13

DATE	EXERCISES TO COMPLETE
	Read pages 217-227 and complete exercises: 4-4 and 4-5

OBJECTIVES

- Exploring the importance of processing anger in recovery work.
- Group processing of anger letters.

NOTES – INSIGHTS – THINGS TO EXPLORE IN THERAPY

ACCOUNTABILITY ISSUES – GOALS FOR THE WEEK

PARTNER RECOVERY GROWTH INDEX (PRGI)

DENIAL | 1 2 3 4 5 6 7 8 9 10

1 = Believing my partner isn't an addict, denying my partner's progress, and/or denying the hurt and pain I am feeling because of my partner's addiction.

10 = Consistently feeling/expressing the pain caused by my partner's behavior and adjusting boundaries when appropriate due to therapeutic insight and progress.

ANXIETY MANAGEMENT | 1 2 3 4 5 6 7 8 9 10

1 = Avoiding anxiety triggers and anxious feelings/sensations in my body

10 = Acknowledging anxiety and using it to provide insight into what is important

ANGER MANAGEMENT | 1 2 3 4 5 6 7 8 9 10

1 = Having explosive outbursts, making threats, yelling, stuffing, devaluing, withholding, and other child-like dynamics when experiencing anger

10 = Consistently expressing anger in an adult-to-adult dynamic and externally processing anger via the use of therapeutic tools

DEPRESSION MANAGEMENT | 1 2 3 4 5 6 7 8 9 10

1 = Choosing to engage in the victim orientation via avoiding emotional processing, not practicing self-care, and self-loathing every day for the past 7+ days

10 = Consistently choosing to use therapeutic tools, practice self-care, and take behavioral baby steps towards one's mission statement in life every day for the past 14 days

SHAME MANAGEMENT | 1 2 3 4 5 6 7 8 9 10

1 = Believing I'm a bad person or a mistake (i.e. I'm a bad wife/I'm unlovable)

10 = Believing I'm a good person who made some mistakes

CO-DEPENDENCY | 1 2 3 4 5 6 7 8 9 10

1 = Exhibiting rescuing behavior, failure to set boundaries, failure to implement consequences for boundary failures, and failing to process one's own issues during the past 7+ days.

10 = I have set/executed boundaries, taken behavioral baby steps towards my individual mission statement, acknowledged/processed my emotions, and living a life that is more internally than externally motivated

BOUNDARIES 1 2 3 4 5 6 7 8 9 10

1 = A total lack of boundaries or the use of vague boundaries to justify withholding.

10 = Consistently maintaining boundaries and implementing consequences when boundaries are violated.

TRUST 1 2 3 4 5 6 7 8 9 10

1 = Obsessing about your partner's recovery (OCD/co-dependency/anxiety), ignoring your partner's recovery work (denial/avoidance) and/or doubting your ability to make good decisions in the past 7+ days

10 = Consistently allowing your boundaries/consequences to work for you, expressing emotions in healthy transparent ways during FANOS check-ins and working towards building healthy attachment.

ACTING-IN 1 2 3 4 5 6 7 8 9 10

1 = I withheld emotional/spiritual/physical intimacy in the past 7 days

10 = 6+ months of continuous emotional/spiritual/physical engagement

FORGIVENESS 1 2 3 4 5 6 7 8 9 10

1 = Holding onto anger/resentment/bitterness and refusing to consider forgiveness

10 = I have fully processed my grief, accepted the betrayal, set boundaries, and reached a level of peace due to forgiveness

CONFLICT RESOLUTION 1 2 3 4 5 6 7 8 9 10

1 = Displaying parent-to-child or child-to-child dynamics during conflict or avoiding conflict via people pleasing behaviors

10 = Consistently using healthy assertiveness and active listening with empathy to resolve conflict or reach a compromise in life every day for the past 14 days

SELF-WORTH 1 2 3 4 5 6 7 8 9 10

1 = Feeling/believing I'm inadequate every day in the past 7+ days

10 = Feeling/believing I'm an adequate individual whose worth is not tied to another individual's behavior each day for the past 3+ months

SELF-CARE 1 2 3 4 5 6 7 8 9 10

1 = Neglecting self-care behaviors/No self-care behaviors during the past 7+ days

10 = Consistently practicing self-care behaviors each day for the past year

Anger's Influence in Partner's Recovery

As the psychological barrier of denial begins to recede, anger quickly surfaces to protect an individual from the threat(s) associated with addiction betrayal. In chapter 1, we explored the fight or flight response to trauma and how fight is a natural response to a threat. At this point of your recovery in chapter 4, you are likely starting to experience an increase in anger and sadness associated with your partner's addiction. The previous exercises were designed to expedite this process by breaking through any denial that might be preventing you from experiencing healthy anger and sadness regarding your present reality. These emotions are healthy when properly processed. However, a lot of people view anger as a negative emotion that cannot be expressed or should not be felt. This is unhealthy when dealing with partner betrayal as anger has a tendency to "boomerang" back to the individual experiencing it. Thus, the anger is turned inward, and this response can lead to a sense of helplessness, powerlessness, and eventually depression. This emotional state can inhibit your therapeutic progress and is toxic because you are not the reason your partner struggles with acting out/acting in behavior. Treatment for internalized anger is external processing and identifying the emotions behind the anger. Physically processing the anger towards a healthy external target can assist in identifying the emotions beneath the fight response. Unhealthy externalization can be identified by the following behaviors: yelling at your partner, slamming doors around the house, shaming your partner for their past mistakes, yelling at your kids and or coworkers due to a present trigger, throwing/breaking things in a non-therapeutic setting, self-harming behaviors, etc. Your anger is valid, but how you process it is the key to working through your grief in a healthy way. Thus, we must externally process the anger towards the sole reason you are in this group: sexual acting out/acting in behavior and the choice of your partner to engage in that behavior. The following exercises can leave you in a raw, emotional state so make sure you allocate appropriate time and space to properly complete the exercises without distractions.

EXERCISE 4-4: EXTERNALIZING ANGER: ACTING OUT/ACTING IN

In this exercise you will write an anger letter to sexual acting out/acting in behavior. The purpose of this letter to is unapologetically tell sexual acting out/acting in behavior how it has damaged your life. Do not pull any punches and allow yourself to tap into any repressed anger that you have been carrying since discovering the presence of acting out/acting in behavior in your relationship. Close the letter by telling Sexual Acting out/Acting in why it will no longer control you anymore.

Dear Sexual Acting out/Acting in,

_____

_____

_____

_____

_____

_____

_____

Sincerely,

EXERCISE 4-5: EXTERNALIZING ANGER: YOUR PARTNER

In this exercise you will write an anger letter to your partner for choosing to act out/act in sexually. THEY ARE NOT TO SEE THIS LETTER. YOU WILL WRITE A SEPARATE LETTER TO SHARE WITH THEM IN A FUTURE EXERCISE. The purpose of this letter to is unapologetically tell your partner how their behavior has damaged your life. Do not pull any punches and allow yourself to tap into any repressed anger that you have been carrying since discovering the presence of acting out/acting in behavior in your relationship.

Dear _____,

_____

_____

_____

_____

_____

_____

_____

Sincerely,

Week 14

DATE	EXERCISES TO COMPLETE
	Read pages 228-251 and complete exercises: 4-6 and 4-7

OBJECTIVES

- Exploring the emotions behind the anger you feel related to your partner's betrayal.
- Group processing of the Anger Iceberg.

NOTES – INSIGHTS – THINGS TO EXPLORE IN THERAPY

ACCOUNTABILITY ISSUES – GOALS FOR THE WEEK

PARTNER RECOVERY GROWTH INDEX (PRGI)

DENIAL   1 2 3 4 5 6 7 8 9 10

1 = Believing my partner isn't an addict, denying my partner's progress, and/or denying the hurt and pain I am feeling because of my partner's addiction.

10 = Consistently feeling/expressing the pain caused by my partner's behavior and adjusting boundaries when appropriate due to therapeutic insight and progress.

ANXIETY MANAGEMENT   1 2 3 4 5 6 7 8 9 10

1 = Avoiding anxiety triggers and anxious feelings/sensations in my body

10 = Acknowledging anxiety and using it to provide insight into what is important

ANGER MANAGEMENT   1 2 3 4 5 6 7 8 9 10

1 = Having explosive outbursts, making threats, yelling, stuffing, devaluing, withholding, and other child-like dynamics when experiencing anger

10 = Consistently expressing anger in an adult-to-adult dynamic and externally processing anger via the use of therapeutic tools

DEPRESSION MANAGEMENT   1 2 3 4 5 6 7 8 9 10

1 = Choosing to engage in the victim orientation via avoiding emotional processing, not practicing self-care, and self-loathing every day for the past 7+ days

10 = Consistently choosing to use therapeutic tools, practice self-care, and take behavioral baby steps towards one's mission statement in life every day for the past 14 days

SHAME MANAGEMENT   1 2 3 4 5 6 7 8 9 10

1 = Believing I'm a bad person or a mistake (i.e. I'm a bad wife/I'm unlovable)

10 = Believing I'm a good person who made some mistakes

CO-DEPENDENCY   1 2 3 4 5 6 7 8 9 10

1 = Exhibiting rescuing behavior, failure to set boundaries, failure to implement consequences for boundary failures, and failing to process one's own issues during the past 7+ days.

10 = I have set/executed boundaries, taken behavioral baby steps towards my individual mission statement, acknowledged/processed my emotions, and living a life that is more internally than externally motivated

BOUNDARIES | 1 2 3 4 5 6 7 8 9 10

1 = A total lack of boundaries or the use of vague boundaries to justify withholding.

10 = Consistently maintaining boundaries and implementing consequences when boundaries are violated.

TRUST | 1 2 3 4 5 6 7 8 9 10

1 = Obsessing about your partner's recovery (OCD/co-dependency/anxiety), ignoring your partner's recovery work (denial/avoidance) and/or doubting your ability to make good decisions in the past 7+ days

10 = Consistently allowing your boundaries/consequences to work for you, expressing emotions in healthy transparent ways during FANOS check-ins and working towards building healthy attachment.

ACTING-IN | 1 2 3 4 5 6 7 8 9 10

1 = I withheld emotional/spiritual/physical intimacy in the past 7 days

10 = 6+ months of continuous emotional/spiritual/physical engagement

FORGIVENESS | 1 2 3 4 5 6 7 8 9 10

1 = Holding onto anger/resentment/bitterness and refusing to consider forgiveness

10 = I have fully processed my grief, accepted the betrayal, set boundaries, and reached a level of peace due to forgiveness

CONFLICT RESOLUTION | 1 2 3 4 5 6 7 8 9 10

1 = Displaying parent-to-child or child-to-child dynamics during conflict or avoiding conflict via people pleasing behaviors

10 = Consistently using healthy assertiveness and active listening with empathy to resolve conflict or reach a compromise in life every day for the past 14 days

SELF-WORTH | 1 2 3 4 5 6 7 8 9 10

1 = Feeling/believing I'm inadequate every day in the past 7+ days

10 = Feeling/believing I'm an adequate individual whose worth is not tied to another individual's behavior each day for the past 3+ months

SELF-CARE | 1 2 3 4 5 6 7 8 9 10

1 = Neglecting self-care behaviors/No self-care behaviors during the past 7+ days

10 = Consistently practicing self-care behaviors each day for the past year

EXERCISE 4-6: ICEBERG OF ANGER

As you know icebergs are a beautiful sight and the reality is we just see the tip of it. In the space provided, draw a picture of an iceberg. Draw a line through the top portion of it. Then place the word anger in the top portion of the iceberg. From there think about all the emotions that are associated with your anger. Place them in the portion of the iceberg that is underneath the surface of your anger. The purpose of this exercise is to identify the emotions that are underneath the surface of your anger. You may want to refer to your anger letters or the wheel of emotions to help you identify the emotions you get to place in this iceberg.

EXERCISE 4-6: ICEBERG OF ANGER

EXERCISE 4-7: EXPLORING THE EMOTIONS BENEATH YOUR ANGER

The purpose of this exercise is to have you take a deeper look at the emotions underneath the surface of your anger. From your anger iceberg please take each emotion and answer the following questions:

Emotion # 1 _____

In what ways does this emotion give power to your anger?

_____

_____

What are some places or situations that elicit this emotion to fuel your anger? Why?

_____

_____

How has anger helped protect you from this emotion?

_____

_____

What have been the negative impacts from expressing this emotion from a place of anger?

_____

_____

Given the negative impacts of your anger. What are some healthy ways to express this emotion that lies beneath your anger?

_____

_____

Emotion # 2 _____

In what ways does this emotion give power to your anger?

_____

_____

What are some places or situations that elicit this emotion to fuel your anger? Why?

_____

_____

How has anger helped protect you from this emotion?

_____

_____

What have been the negative impacts from expressing this emotion from a place of anger?

_____

_____

Given the negative impacts of your anger. What are some healthy ways to express this emotion that lies beneath your anger?

_____

_____

Emotion # 3 _____

In what ways does this emotion give power to your anger?

_____

_____

What are some places or situations that elicit this emotion to fuel your anger? Why?

_____

_____

How has anger helped protect you from this emotion?

_____

_____

What have been the negative impacts from expressing this emotion from a place of anger?

_____

_____

Given the negative impacts of your anger. What are some healthy ways to express this emotion that lies beneath your anger?

Emotion # 4 _____

In what ways does this emotion give power to your anger?

_____

_____

What are some places or situations that elicit this emotion to fuel your anger? Why?

_____

_____

How has anger helped protect you from this emotion?

_____

_____

What have been the negative impacts from expressing this emotion from a place of anger?

_____

_____

Given the negative impacts of your anger. What are some healthy ways to express this emotion that lies beneath your anger?

_____

_____

Emotion # 5 _____

In what ways does this emotion give power to your anger?

_____

_____

What are some places or situations that elicit this emotion to fuel your anger? Why?

_____

_____

How has anger helped protect you from this emotion?

What have been the negative impacts from expressing this emotion from a place of anger?

Given the negative impacts of your anger. What are some healthy ways to express this emotion that lies beneath your anger?

Emotion # 6 _____

In what ways does this emotion give power to your anger?

What are some places or situations that elicit this emotion to fuel your anger? Why?

How has anger helped protect you from this emotion?

What have been the negative impacts from expressing this emotion from a place of anger?

Given the negative impacts of your anger. What are some healthy ways to express this emotion that lies beneath your anger?

Emotion # 7_____

In what ways does this emotion give power to your anger?

_____

_____

What are some places or situations that elicit this emotion to fuel your anger? Why?

_____

_____

How has anger helped protect you from this emotion?

_____

_____

What have been the negative impacts from expressing this emotion from a place of anger?

_____

_____

Given the negative impacts of your anger. What are some healthy ways to express this emotion that lies beneath your anger?

Emotion # 8 _____

In what ways does this emotion give power to your anger?

What are some places or situations that elicit this emotion to fuel your anger? Why?

How has anger helped protect you from this emotion?

What have been the negative impacts from expressing this emotion from a place of anger?

_____

_____

Given the negative impacts of your anger. What are some healthy ways to express this emotion that lies beneath your anger?

_____

_____

Emotion # 9 _____

In what ways does this emotion give power to your anger?

_____

_____

What are some places or situations that elicit this emotion to fuel your anger? Why?

_____

_____

How has anger helped protect you from this emotion?

_____

_____

What have been the negative impacts from expressing this emotion from a place of anger?

_____

_____

Given the negative impacts of your anger. What are some healthy ways to express this emotion that lies beneath your anger?

_____

_____

Emotion # 10 _____

In what ways does this emotion give power to your anger?

_____

_____

What are some places or situations that elicit this emotion to fuel your anger? Why?

How has anger helped protect you from this emotion?

_____

_____

What have been the negative impacts from expressing this emotion from a place of anger?

_____

_____

Given the negative impacts of your anger. What are some healthy ways to express this emotion that lies beneath your anger?

_____

_____

Emotion # 11_____

In what ways does this emotion give power to your anger?

What are some places or situations that elicit this emotion to fuel your anger? Why?

How has anger helped protect you from this emotion?

What have been the negative impacts from expressing this emotion from a place of anger?

Given the negative impacts of your anger. What are some healthy ways to express this emotion that lies beneath your anger?

Emotion # 12 _____

In what ways does this emotion give power to your anger?

_____

_____

What are some places or situations that elicit this emotion to fuel your anger? Why?

_____

_____

How has anger helped protect you from this emotion?

_____

_____

What have been the negative impacts from expressing this emotion from a place of anger?

_____

_____

Given the negative impacts of your anger. What are some healthy ways to express this emotion that lies beneath your anger?

Emotion # 13 _____

In what ways does this emotion give power to your anger?

What are some places or situations that elicit this emotion to fuel your anger? Why?

How has anger helped protect you from this emotion?

What have been the negative impacts from expressing this emotion from a place of anger?

Given the negative impacts of your anger. What are some healthy ways to express this emotion that lies beneath your anger?

Emotion # 14 _____

In what ways does this emotion give power to your anger?

What are some places or situations that elicit this emotion to fuel your anger? Why?

How has anger helped protect you from this emotion?

_____

_____

What have been the negative impacts from expressing this emotion from a place of anger?

_____

_____

Given the negative impacts of your anger. What are some healthy ways to express this emotion that lies beneath your anger?

_____

_____

Emotion # 15_____

In what ways does this emotion give power to your anger?

_____

_____

What are some places or situations that elicit this emotion to fuel your anger? Why?

_____

_____

How has anger helped protect you from this emotion?

_____

_____

What have been the negative impacts from expressing this emotion from a place of anger?

_____

_____

Given the negative impacts of your anger. What are some healthy ways to express this emotion that lies beneath your anger?

_____

_____

Week 15

DATE	EXERCISES TO COMPLETE
	Read pages 252-257 and complete exercise: 4-8

OBJECTIVES

- Exploring the origins and consequences of resentment.
- Group processing of the Resentment Tree.

NOTES – INSIGHTS – THINGS TO EXPLORE IN THERAPY

ACCOUNTABILITY ISSUES – GOALS FOR THE WEEK

PARTNER RECOVERY GROWTH INDEX (PRGI)

DENIAL   1 2 3 4 5 6 7 8 9 10

1 = Believing my partner isn't an addict, denying my partner's progress, and/or denying the hurt and pain I am feeling because of my partner's addiction.

10 = Consistently feeling/expressing the pain caused by my partner's behavior and adjusting boundaries when appropriate due to therapeutic insight and progress.

ANXIETY MANAGEMENT   1 2 3 4 5 6 7 8 9 10

1 = Avoiding anxiety triggers and anxious feelings/sensations in my body

10 = Acknowledging anxiety and using it to provide insight into what is important

ANGER MANAGEMENT   1 2 3 4 5 6 7 8 9 10

1 = Having explosive outbursts, making threats, yelling, stuffing, devaluing, withholding, and other child-like dynamics when experiencing anger

10 = Consistently expressing anger in an adult-to-adult dynamic and externally processing anger via the use of therapeutic tools

DEPRESSION MANAGEMENT   1 2 3 4 5 6 7 8 9 10

1 = Choosing to engage in the victim orientation via avoiding emotional processing, not practicing self-care, and self-loathing every day for the past 7+ days

10 = Consistently choosing to use therapeutic tools, practice self-care, and take behavioral baby steps towards one's mission statement in life every day for the past 14 days

SHAME MANAGEMENT   1 2 3 4 5 6 7 8 9 10

1 = Believing I'm a bad person or a mistake (i.e. I'm a bad wife/I'm unlovable)

10 = Believing I'm a good person who made some mistakes

CO-DEPENDENCY   1 2 3 4 5 6 7 8 9 10

1 = Exhibiting rescuing behavior, failure to set boundaries, failure to implement consequences for boundary failures, and failing to process one's own issues during the past 7+ days.

10 = I have set/executed boundaries, taken behavioral baby steps towards my individual mission statement, acknowledged/processed my emotions, and living a life that is more internally than externally motivated

BOUNDARIES | 1 2 3 4 5 6 7 8 9 10

1 = A total lack of boundaries or the use of vague boundaries to justify withholding.

10 = Consistently maintaining boundaries and implementing consequences when boundaries are violated.

TRUST | 1 2 3 4 5 6 7 8 9 10

1 = Obsessing about your partner's recovery (OCD/co-dependency/anxiety), ignoring your partner's recovery work (denial/avoidance) and/or doubting your ability to make good decisions in the past 7+ days

10 = Consistently allowing your boundaries/consequences to work for you, expressing emotions in healthy transparent ways during FANOS check-ins and working towards building healthy attachment.

ACTING-IN | 1 2 3 4 5 6 7 8 9 10

1 = I withheld emotional/spiritual/physical intimacy in the past 7 days

10 = 6+ months of continuous emotional/spiritual/physical engagement

FORGIVENESS | 1 2 3 4 5 6 7 8 9 10

1 = Holding onto anger/resentment/bitterness and refusing to consider forgiveness

10 = I have fully processed my grief, accepted the betrayal, set boundaries, and reached a level of peace due to forgiveness

CONFLICT RESOLUTION | 1 2 3 4 5 6 7 8 9 10

1 = Displaying parent-to-child or child-to-child dynamics during conflict or avoiding conflict via people pleasing behaviors

10 = Consistently using healthy assertiveness and active listening with empathy to resolve conflict or reach a compromise in life every day for the past 14 days

SELF-WORTH | 1 2 3 4 5 6 7 8 9 10

1 = Feeling/believing I'm inadequate every day in the past 7+ days

10 = Feeling/believing I'm an adequate individual whose worth is not tied to another individual's behavior each day for the past 3+ months

SELF-CARE | 1 2 3 4 5 6 7 8 9 10

1 = Neglecting self-care behaviors/No self-care behaviors during the past 7+ days

10 = Consistently practicing self-care behaviors each day for the past year

Resentment

Now that you have gotten in touch with your anger and the emotions beneath your anger, you have likely identified resentment as an emotion to be therapeutically processed. Resentment is often the product of multiple experiences where anger was present but never completely addressed via healthy conflict resolution. In your present reality, resentment is likely the product of reflecting on all the times your partner was knowingly acting out/acting in while you were committed to fidelity. It's not like his or her behavior was an honest mistake, despite the role denial was playing in his or her life. Your partner chose to act out/act in despite the risks to hurting you, themselves, and your family. This is not something that is easy to accept, and holding on to resentment is a way to punish your partner for what they have done. If you are desiring to reconcile in your relationship, addressing resentment and all the behaviors that are a result of resentment is critical to your recovery. After all, how can you expect your partner to desire to connect with you if he or she knows you are harboring resentment towards them? Remember, they also struggle with a fear of intimacy. Thus, if connection is your desire, you get to work through your resentment.

EXERCISE 4-8: TREE OF RESENTMENT

In the space below, draw a picture of a giant tree with the following traits: root system, trunk, and a giant leafy/branch canopy. Label the trunk as "Resentment." Label the individual roots with the thoughts, emotions, and experiences that nourish resentment in your life. Now in the canopy, fill the tree with all the behaviors that manifest in your life and relationship due to your resentment. You can think of these things as the produce associated with your tree of resentment. As you sit back and look at your tree, ask yourself if this is the type of behavior you want to produce in your life and relationship. The purpose of this exercise is not to shame you for how resentment has manifested in your life. The purpose is to help you identify the importance of processing your anger in healthy ways and how unprocessed anger has separated or is separating you from who you really are as a person. Process your tree with your therapist and clinician-lead group.

EXERCISE 4-8: TREE OF RESENTMENT

Week 16

DATE	EXERCISES TO COMPLETE
	Read pages 258-269 and complete exercises: 4-9 and 4-10

OBJECTIVES

- Grieving the losses related to your partner's acting out/acting in behavior.
- Group processing of grief and exploring a pathway to healing.

NOTES – INSIGHTS – THINGS TO EXPLORE IN THERAPY

ACCOUNTABILITY ISSUES – GOALS FOR THE WEEK

PARTNER RECOVERY GROWTH INDEX (PRGI)

DENIAL 1 2 3 4 5 6 7 8 9 10

1 = Believing my partner isn't an addict, denying my partner's progress, and/or denying the hurt and pain I am feeling because of my partner's addiction.

10 = Consistently feeling/expressing the pain caused by my partner's behavior and adjusting boundaries when appropriate due to therapeutic insight and progress.

ANXIETY MANAGEMENT 1 2 3 4 5 6 7 8 9 10

1 = Avoiding anxiety triggers and anxious feelings/sensations in my body

10 = Acknowledging anxiety and using it to provide insight into what is important

ANGER MANAGEMENT 1 2 3 4 5 6 7 8 9 10

1 = Having explosive outbursts, making threats, yelling, stuffing, devaluing, withholding, and other child-like dynamics when experiencing anger

10 = Consistently expressing anger in an adult-to-adult dynamic and externally processing anger via the use of therapeutic tools

DEPRESSION MANAGEMENT 1 2 3 4 5 6 7 8 9 10

1 = Choosing to engage in the victim orientation via avoiding emotional processing, not practicing self-care, and self-loathing every day for the past 7+ days

10 = Consistently choosing to use therapeutic tools, practice self-care, and take behavioral baby steps towards one's mission statement in life every day for the past 14 days

SHAME MANAGEMENT 1 2 3 4 5 6 7 8 9 10

1 = Believing I'm a bad person or a mistake (i.e. I'm a bad wife/I'm unlovable)

10 = Believing I'm a good person who made some mistakes

CO-DEPENDENCY 1 2 3 4 5 6 7 8 9 10

1 = Exhibiting rescuing behavior, failure to set boundaries, failure to implement consequences for boundary failures, and failing to process one's own issues during the past 7+ days.

10 = I have set/executed boundaries, taken behavioral baby steps towards my individual mission statement, acknowledged/processed my emotions, and living a life that is more internally than externally motivated

BOUNDARIES | 1 2 3 4 5 6 7 8 9 10

1 = A total lack of boundaries or the use of vague boundaries to justify withholding.

10 = Consistently maintaining boundaries and implementing consequences when boundaries are violated.

TRUST | 1 2 3 4 5 6 7 8 9 10

1 = Obsessing about your partner's recovery (OCD/co-dependency/anxiety), ignoring your partner's recovery work (denial/avoidance) and/or doubting your ability to make good decisions in the past 7+ days

10 = Consistently allowing your boundaries/consequences to work for you, expressing emotions in healthy transparent ways during FANOS check-ins and working towards building healthy attachment.

ACTING-IN | 1 2 3 4 5 6 7 8 9 10

1 = I withheld emotional/spiritual/physical intimacy in the past 7 days

10 = 6+ months of continuous emotional/spiritual/physical engagement

FORGIVENESS | 1 2 3 4 5 6 7 8 9 10

1 = Holding onto anger/resentment/bitterness and refusing to consider forgiveness

10 = I have fully processed my grief, accepted the betrayal, set boundaries, and reached a level of peace due to forgiveness

CONFLICT RESOLUTION | 1 2 3 4 5 6 7 8 9 10

1 = Displaying parent-to-child or child-to-child dynamics during conflict or avoiding conflict via people pleasing behaviors

10 = Consistently using healthy assertiveness and active listening with empathy to resolve conflict or reach a compromise in life every day for the past 14 days

SELF-WORTH | 1 2 3 4 5 6 7 8 9 10

1 = Feeling/believing I'm inadequate every day in the past 7+ days

10 = Feeling/believing I'm an adequate individual whose worth is not tied to another individual's behavior each day for the past 3+ months

SELF-CARE | 1 2 3 4 5 6 7 8 9 10

1 = Neglecting self-care behaviors/No self-care behaviors during the past 7+ days

10 = Consistently practicing self-care behaviors each day for the past year

Sadness

When completing your anger iceberg, you probably noticed multiple feelings associated with sadness underneath your anger. As you begin to process your anger and resentment, sadness often surfaces somatically and emotionally. Sometimes after physical processing during anger work, clients break down into crying spells as a feeling of heaviness overcomes their bodies. This is normal and an indication of deep sadness. For clients that struggle with emotional vulnerability, they may notice tension in their throats that eventually moves behind their eyes. This is their body telling them that sadness gets to be released or shared in the moment. Sadness doesn't mean that you are weak. It simply indicates that you have experienced some sort of loss that is meaningful to you in your life. If you think back to chapter 1 on how anger can be the protective product of a trauma-related fight response, we can now see that there wasn't any time for experiencing total sadness while anger was shielding you from your pain. Now, we begin the process of acknowledging your sadness related to the losses associated with your partner's acting out/acting in behavior. It is paramount that you don't hold your sadness inside over the next few weeks/months of processing.

Withholding your sadness will often lead to isolation. Depression symptoms can manifest if you don't co-regulate and process what you are feeling. That is why group processing of your pain with individuals who can relate to betrayal due to acting out/acting in behavior is key in reducing your shame and sadness. You are not alone and your sadness matters. Even if your partner is not at a place of validating your pain and suffering due to their behavior, you can validate your pain and suffering internally and externally with the people in your group.

EXERCISE 4-9: INVENTORY OF LOSSES

In exercise 4-1, you listed the top 40 impacts of your partner's addiction in your life. Some of those impacts were likely losses. In this exercise, you will list all the losses you have experienced as a result of your partner's addiction.

Example: "I lost my self-confidence regarding my appearance."

"I lost my ability to trust my partner with finances."

"I lost my ability to trust my own intuition."

"I lost time of unfulfilled emotional intimacy."

1._____

2._____

3._____

4._____

5._____

6._____

7._____

8.
9.
10.
11.
12.
13.
14.
15.
16.
17.
18.
19.
20.
21.
22.

23._____

24._____

25._____

26._____

27._____

28._____

29._____

30._____

EXERCISE 4-10: REFLECTION ON INVENTORY OF LOSSES

Now that you have taken an inventory of the losses associated with your partner's acting-out/acting-in behavior, answer the following questions.

1. What losses on your list are the most painful?_____

_____

_____

_____

2. What losses on the list are permanent? What can you do to move towards accepting the loss and moving towards healing in your life?

Loss:_____

Path towards acceptance/healing: _____

_____

_____

_____

EXERCISE 4-10: REFLECTION ON INVENTORY OF LOSSES

Loss:_____

Path towards acceptance/healing:_____

_____

_____

_____

Loss:_____

Path towards acceptance/healing:_____

_____

_____

_____

Loss:_____

Path towards acceptance/healing:_____

_____

_____

_____

3. What losses on the list are not permanent? What can you do to move towards accepting the loss and moving towards healing in your life?

Loss:_____

Path towards acceptance/healing: _____

_____

_____

_____

Loss:_____

Path towards acceptance/healing: _____

_____

_____

_____

Loss:_____

Path towards acceptance/healing: _____

_____

_____

_____

Loss:_____

Path towards acceptance/healing:_____

_____

_____

_____

Loss:_____

Path towards acceptance/healing:_____

_____

_____

_____

4. What are your biggest insights from the completion of this exercise? _____

_____

_____

_____

_____

Week 17

DATE	EXERCISES TO COMPLETE
	Read pages 270-277 and complete exercises: 4-11 and 4-12

OBJECTIVES

- Exploring the importance of acceptance.
- Group processing of what acceptance looks like for you.

NOTES – INSIGHTS – THINGS TO EXPLORE IN THERAPY

ACCOUNTABILITY ISSUES – GOALS FOR THE WEEK

PARTNER RECOVERY GROWTH INDEX (PRGI)

DENIAL   1 2 3 4 5 6 7 8 9 10

1 = Believing my partner isn't an addict, denying my partner's progress, and/or denying the hurt and pain I am feeling because of my partner's addiction.

10 = Consistently feeling/expressing the pain caused by my partner's behavior and adjusting boundaries when appropriate due to therapeutic insight and progress.

ANXIETY MANAGEMENT   1 2 3 4 5 6 7 8 9 10

1 = Avoiding anxiety triggers and anxious feelings/sensations in my body

10 = Acknowledging anxiety and using it to provide insight into what is important

ANGER MANAGEMENT   1 2 3 4 5 6 7 8 9 10

1 = Having explosive outbursts, making threats, yelling, stuffing, devaluing, withholding, and other child-like dynamics when experiencing anger

10 = Consistently expressing anger in an adult-to-adult dynamic and externally processing anger via the use of therapeutic tools

DEPRESSION MANAGEMENT   1 2 3 4 5 6 7 8 9 10

1 = Choosing to engage in the victim orientation via avoiding emotional processing, not practicing self-care, and self-loathing every day for the past 7+ days

10 = Consistently choosing to use therapeutic tools, practice self-care, and take behavioral baby steps towards one's mission statement in life every day for the past 14 days

SHAME MANAGEMENT   1 2 3 4 5 6 7 8 9 10

1 = Believing I'm a bad person or a mistake (i.e. I'm a bad wife/I'm unlovable)

10 = Believing I'm a good person who made some mistakes

CO-DEPENDENCY   1 2 3 4 5 6 7 8 9 10

1 = Exhibiting rescuing behavior, failure to set boundaries, failure to implement consequences for boundary failures, and failing to process one's own issues during the past 7+ days.

10 = I have set/executed boundaries, taken behavioral baby steps towards my individual mission statement, acknowledged/processed my emotions, and living a life that is more internally than externally motivated

BOUNDARIES 1 2 3 4 5 6 7 8 9 10

1 = A total lack of boundaries or the use of vague boundaries to justify withholding.

10 = Consistently maintaining boundaries and implementing consequences when boundaries are violated.

TRUST 1 2 3 4 5 6 7 8 9 10

1 = Obsessing about your partner's recovery (OCD/co-dependency/anxiety), ignoring your partner's recovery work (denial/avoidance) and/or doubting your ability to make good decisions in the past 7+ days

10 = Consistently allowing your boundaries/consequences to work for you, expressing emotions in healthy transparent ways during FANOS check-ins and working towards building healthy attachment.

ACTING-IN 1 2 3 4 5 6 7 8 9 10

1 = I withheld emotional/spiritual/physical intimacy in the past 7 days

10 = 6+ months of continuous emotional/spiritual/physical engagement

FORGIVENESS 1 2 3 4 5 6 7 8 9 10

1 = Holding onto anger/resentment/bitterness and refusing to consider forgiveness

10 = I have fully processed my grief, accepted the betrayal, set boundaries, and reached a level of peace due to forgiveness

CONFLICT RESOLUTION 1 2 3 4 5 6 7 8 9 10

1 = Displaying parent-to-child or child-to-child dynamics during conflict or avoiding conflict via people pleasing behaviors

10 = Consistently using healthy assertiveness and active listening with empathy to resolve conflict or reach a compromise in life every day for the past 14 days

SELF-WORTH 1 2 3 4 5 6 7 8 9 10

1 = Feeling/believing I'm inadequate every day in the past 7+ days

10 = Feeling/believing I'm an adequate individual whose worth is not tied to another individual's behavior each day for the past 3+ months

SELF-CARE 1 2 3 4 5 6 7 8 9 10

1 = Neglecting self-care behaviors/No self-care behaviors during the past 7+ days

10 = Consistently practicing self-care behaviors each day for the past year

EXERCISE 4-11: DIALOGUE WITH ACCEPTANCE

In this exercise, you will write a letter to a future version of yourself who has reached acceptance concerning your partner's acting out/acting in addiction/behaviors. In the letter, discuss the progress you have made, and explore all the feelings, questions, and issues you have on the table that are limiting your ability to get to that place of acceptance.

Dear _____,

_____

_____

_____

_____

_____

_____

_____

_____

EXERCISE 4-11: DIALOGUE WITH ACCEPTANCE

Sincerely,

EXERCISE 4-12: MOVING TOWARDS ACCEPTANCE

Now that you have identified your progress in grieving the losses in your relationship and identified issues on the table, take a moment to answer the following questions below. The purpose of this exercise is to develop an action plan for continuing to progress towards acceptance.

1. What is the main issue that is currently keeping me stuck in my grief? _____

_____

2. What steps have I already taken to address this issue? _____

_____

_____

3. What additional steps can I take to address this issue? _____

_____

_____

_____

4. Who can help hold me accountable for taking these actions steps?

Person #1: _____ Person #2: _____

EXERCISE 4-12: MOVING TOWARDS ACCEPTANCE

5. What is another issue that is currently keeping me stuck in my grief?

_____

_____

6. What steps have I already taken to address this issue? _____

_____

_____

7. What additional steps can I take to address this issue? _____

_____

_____

_____

8. Who can help hold me accountable for taking these actions steps?

Person #1: _____ Person #2: _____

9. What is another issue that is currently keeping me stuck in my grief?

_____

_____

10. What steps have I already taken to address this issue? _____

_____

_____

11. What additional steps can I take to address this issue? _____

_____

_____

12. Who can hold me accountable for taking these actions steps?

Person #1: _____ Person #2: _____

I agree to work the action plan steps in this exercise to move towards acceptance and I will use my accountability partners for accountability during this process. If I fail to apply these actions steps, I will process my resistance with my therapist/life coach.

Signed: _____ **Date:** _____

Week 18

DATE	EXERCISES TO COMPLETE
	Read pages 278-288 and complete exercise: 5-1

OBJECTIVES

- Exploring the Drama Triangle.
- Group processing of your role in the Drama Triangle.

NOTES – INSIGHTS – THINGS TO EXPLORE IN THERAPY

ACCOUNTABILITY ISSUES – GOALS FOR THE WEEK

PARTNER RECOVERY GROWTH INDEX (PRGI)

DENIAL 1 2 3 4 5 6 7 8 9 10

1 = Believing my partner isn't an addict, denying my partner's progress, and/or denying the hurt and pain I am feeling because of my partner's addiction.

10 = Consistently feeling/expressing the pain caused by my partner's behavior and adjusting boundaries when appropriate due to therapeutic insight and progress.

ANXIETY MANAGEMENT 1 2 3 4 5 6 7 8 9 10

1 = Avoiding anxiety triggers and anxious feelings/sensations in my body

10 = Acknowledging anxiety and using it to provide insight into what is important

ANGER MANAGEMENT 1 2 3 4 5 6 7 8 9 10

1 = Having explosive outbursts, making threats, yelling, stuffing, devaluing, withholding, and other child-like dynamics when experiencing anger

10 = Consistently expressing anger in an adult-to-adult dynamic and externally processing anger via the use of therapeutic tools

DEPRESSION MANAGEMENT 1 2 3 4 5 6 7 8 9 10

1 = Choosing to engage in the victim orientation via avoiding emotional processing, not practicing self-care, and self-loathing every day for the past 7+ days

10 = Consistently choosing to use therapeutic tools, practice self-care, and take behavioral baby steps towards one's mission statement in life every day for the past 14 days

SHAME MANAGEMENT 1 2 3 4 5 6 7 8 9 10

1 = Believing I'm a bad person or a mistake (i.e. I'm a bad wife/I'm unlovable)

10 = Believing I'm a good person who made some mistakes

CO-DEPENDENCY 1 2 3 4 5 6 7 8 9 10

1 = Exhibiting rescuing behavior, failure to set boundaries, failure to implement consequences for boundary failures, and failing to process one's own issues during the past 7+ days.

10 = I have set/executed boundaries, taken behavioral baby steps towards my individual mission statement, acknowledged/processed my emotions, and living a life that is more internally than externally motivated

BOUNDARIES | 1 2 3 4 5 6 7 8 9 10

1 = A total lack of boundaries or the use of vague boundaries to justify withholding.

10 = Consistently maintaining boundaries and implementing consequences when boundaries are violated.

TRUST | 1 2 3 4 5 6 7 8 9 10

1 = Obsessing about your partner's recovery (OCD/co-dependency/anxiety), ignoring your partner's recovery work (denial/avoidance) and/or doubting your ability to make good decisions in the past 7+ days

10 = Consistently allowing your boundaries/consequences to work for you, expressing emotions in healthy transparent ways during FANOS check-ins and working towards building healthy attachment.

ACTING-IN | 1 2 3 4 5 6 7 8 9 10

1 = I withheld emotional/spiritual/physical intimacy in the past 7 days

10 = 6+ months of continuous emotional/spiritual/physical engagement

FORGIVENESS | 1 2 3 4 5 6 7 8 9 10

1 = Holding onto anger/resentment/bitterness and refusing to consider forgiveness

10 = I have fully processed my grief, accepted the betrayal, set boundaries, and reached a level of peace due to forgiveness

CONFLICT RESOLUTION | 1 2 3 4 5 6 7 8 9 10

1 = Displaying parent-to-child or child-to-child dynamics during conflict or avoiding conflict via people pleasing behaviors

10 = Consistently using healthy assertiveness and active listening with empathy to resolve conflict or reach a compromise in life every day for the past 14 days

SELF-WORTH | 1 2 3 4 5 6 7 8 9 10

1 = Feeling/believing I'm inadequate every day in the past 7+ days

10 = Feeling/believing I'm an adequate individual whose worth is not tied to another individual's behavior each day for the past 3+ months

SELF-CARE | 1 2 3 4 5 6 7 8 9 10

1 = Neglecting self-care behaviors/No self-care behaviors during the past 7+ days

10 = Consistently practicing self-care behaviors each day for the past year

Chapter 5: Understanding Physical and Relational Dynamics Within an Addictive System

At this point in the recovery process, we have addressed trauma, established self-care, established boundaries, and progressed in the process of grieving concerning your partner's betrayal. Hopefully, your amygdala and sympathetic nervous system are becoming less triggered by your partner's behaviors and your cortex is more receptive to the psychoeducational aspects of your recovery. In this chapter, we will explore concepts associated with the addictive system and how you have played a willing or unwilling role in that system. Understanding and applying these concepts can expedite your individual healing process and the process of relational reconciliation if you are choosing to pursue reconciliation in your recovery. One of the first concepts to explore is the reality that addiction thrives in chaos/drama. An addict MUST have chaos in his or her life to rationalize his or her choice to pursue acting-out/acting-in behavior. One way to achieve such chaos is engagement in what Stephen Karpman called the "Drama Triangle."

Karpman Drama Triangle

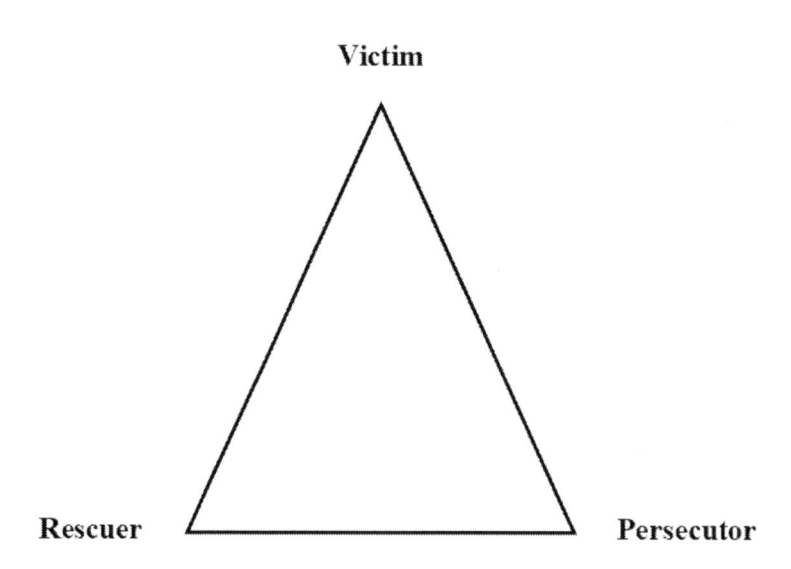

Victim

Rescuer   **Persecutor**

The drama triangle was developed by Stephen Karpman to theoretically explain unhealthy interpersonal dynamics in relationships. The primary roles consist of the Victim, Persecutor, and Rescuer. Victims feel externally controlled by the persecutor or persecutors in their lives and rely on the rescuer to deal with the emotional/circumstantial pain created by the persecutor. In the case of your spouse/partner, he or she had to psychologically make themselves the victim in the drama triangle to justify his or her excuse to use the rescuer of acting-out/acting-in behavior. During this process, you likely felt persecuted by the gaslighting/irrational behaviors exhibited toward you in your relationship. Thus, you felt like a victim of your spouse/partner or his or her addiction. At some point, you may have felt responsible for rescuing your spouse/partner from his or her addiction and identified as a rescuer in the drama triangle while viewing your spouse/partner's acting-out/acting-in behavior as the persecutor in the drama. These patterns of engagement in the drama must be addressed for you and your relationship to heal. Understanding your role in the drama and setting boundaries with victim, persecutor, and rescuer behaviors are critical to developing healthy attachment in relationships. Transactional Analysis (TA) uses the drama triangle to analyze unhealthy transactions, or behavioral verbal/non-verbal behavioral interactions, between people in relationships to understand individual contributions to the drama triangle in your life. Through this methodology, we can identify co-dependent behaviors, develop healthier communication skills, and learn how our inner-child and inner-parent influence our attachment with others.

EXERCISE 5-1: WHAT IS MY ROLE IN THE DRAMA?

Reflect on the drawing below while answering the following questions. Consider how you shift roles in your relationship with your spouse/partner and with others in your life.

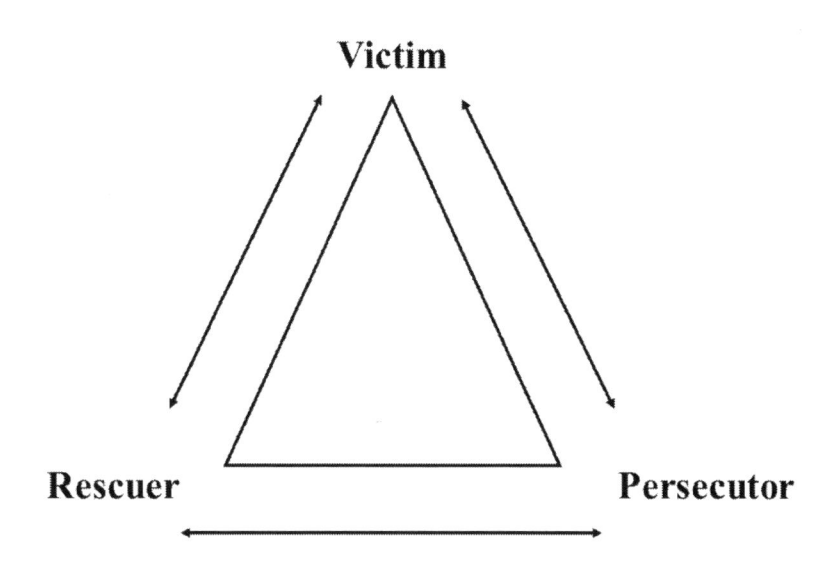

Victim

Rescuer **Persecutor**

1. What is your primary role in the drama triangle? What are some examples of engagement in the drama triangle with your partner?

_____

_____

_____

_____

2. How are you the rescuer in the relationship with your partner?

3. How is your partner's acting-out/acting-in behavior your persecutor?

4. How are you currently playing the victim in your relationship?

5. How is maintaining a victim mentality impacting your recovery?

6. How are you the persecutor of yourself?

7. What are some steps you can take to disengage the drama triangle in your life and relationships?

Week 19

DATE	EXERCISES TO COMPLETE
	Read pages 289-304 and complete exercises: 5-2, 5-3, and 5-4

OBJECTIVES

- Exploring the FANOS relationship check-in recovery tool.
- Group processing of communication strategies for disengaging the Drama Triangle.

NOTES – INSIGHTS – THINGS TO EXPLORE IN THERAPY

ACCOUNTABILITY ISSUES – GOALS FOR THE WEEK

PARTNER RECOVERY GROWTH INDEX (PRGI)

DENIAL | 1 2 3 4 5 6 7 8 9 10

1 = Believing my partner isn't an addict, denying my partner's progress, and/or denying the hurt and pain I am feeling because of my partner's addiction.

10 = Consistently feeling/expressing the pain caused by my partner's behavior and adjusting boundaries when appropriate due to therapeutic insight and progress.

ANXIETY MANAGEMENT | 1 2 3 4 5 6 7 8 9 10

1 = Avoiding anxiety triggers and anxious feelings/sensations in my body

10 = Acknowledging anxiety and using it to provide insight into what is important

ANGER MANAGEMENT | 1 2 3 4 5 6 7 8 9 10

1 = Having explosive outbursts, making threats, yelling, stuffing, devaluing, withholding, and other child-like dynamics when experiencing anger

10 = Consistently expressing anger in an adult-to-adult dynamic and externally processing anger via the use of therapeutic tools

DEPRESSION MANAGEMENT | 1 2 3 4 5 6 7 8 9 10

1 = Choosing to engage in the victim orientation via avoiding emotional processing, not practicing self-care, and self-loathing every day for the past 7+ days

10 = Consistently choosing to use therapeutic tools, practice self-care, and take behavioral baby steps towards one's mission statement in life every day for the past 14 days

SHAME MANAGEMENT | 1 2 3 4 5 6 7 8 9 10

1 = Believing I'm a bad person or a mistake (i.e. I'm a bad wife/I'm unlovable)

10 = Believing I'm a good person who made some mistakes

CO-DEPENDENCY | 1 2 3 4 5 6 7 8 9 10

1 = Exhibiting rescuing behavior, failure to set boundaries, failure to implement consequences for boundary failures, and failing to process one's own issues during the past 7+ days.

10 = I have set/executed boundaries, taken behavioral baby steps towards my individual mission statement, acknowledged/processed my emotions, and living a life that is more internally than externally motivated

BOUNDARIES | 1 2 3 4 5 6 7 8 9 10

1 = A total lack of boundaries or the use of vague boundaries to justify withholding.

10 = Consistently maintaining boundaries and implementing consequences when boundaries are violated.

TRUST | 1 2 3 4 5 6 7 8 9 10

1 = Obsessing about your partner's recovery (OCD/co-dependency/anxiety), ignoring your partner's recovery work (denial/avoidance) and/or doubting your ability to make good decisions in the past 7+ days

10 = Consistently allowing your boundaries/consequences to work for you, expressing emotions in healthy transparent ways during FANOS check-ins and working towards building healthy attachment.

ACTING-IN | 1 2 3 4 5 6 7 8 9 10

1 = I withheld emotional/spiritual/physical intimacy in the past 7 days

10 = 6+ months of continuous emotional/spiritual/physical engagement

FORGIVENESS | 1 2 3 4 5 6 7 8 9 10

1 = Holding onto anger/resentment/bitterness and refusing to consider forgiveness

10 = I have fully processed my grief, accepted the betrayal, set boundaries, and reached a level of peace due to forgiveness

CONFLICT RESOLUTION | 1 2 3 4 5 6 7 8 9 10

1 = Displaying parent-to-child or child-to-child dynamics during conflict or avoiding conflict via people pleasing behaviors

10 = Consistently using healthy assertiveness and active listening with empathy to resolve conflict or reach a compromise in life every day for the past 14 days

SELF-WORTH | 1 2 3 4 5 6 7 8 9 10

1 = Feeling/believing I'm inadequate every day in the past 7+ days

10 = Feeling/believing I'm an adequate individual whose worth is not tied to another individual's behavior each day for the past 3+ months

SELF-CARE | 1 2 3 4 5 6 7 8 9 10

1 = Neglecting self-care behaviors/No self-care behaviors during the past 7+ days

10 = Consistently practicing self-care behaviors each day for the past year

How do I get out of the drama? Disengaging the drama triangle requires patience, self-reflection, honesty, and hard work. Sometimes it requires the establishment of new boundaries with oneself or your significant other and becoming comfortable with saying "no" and meaning it. It also requires establishing a goal or goals to pursue instead of focusing on what cannot be changed regarding the past/present. One example I give clients in teaching this concept is the process of driving down a road. If I attempt to drive while looking behind me, the chances are that I am going to crash. However, if I focus on the road in front of me, I can eventually make it to my destination. Establishing a realistic goal for where you want to go in life and taking specific, behavioral steps to continue down that road are the key to disengaging the drama. For example, if I set a goal of learning to communicate and connect with my spouse/partner on an emotional level after betrayal, I wouldn't constantly focus on all the ways they hurt me in the past. This would keep me in a victim mentality with my spouse/partner playing the role of persecutor and my emotional distance playing the role of my rescuer. Instead, I would focus on the behavioral change I am witnessing in my spouse/partner's behavior, his or her compliance concerning my boundaries, and choosing to hold him or her accountable for behaviors moving forward. This keeps you focused on your destination of emotionally attaching again as you begin to lean into your own anxiety to build trust. Mistakes will happen, and choosing to talk through those mistakes with individual ownership while focusing on your relational goals is critical to disengaging the drama triangle. One communication exercise to "check-in" concerning your spouse/partner's recovery, your recovery, and your relational recovery is Debra Laaser's FANOS. The FANOS acronym stands for feelings, affirmations, needs, ownership, and sobriety. When you are ready to begin the process of ending the drama triangle in your relationship and reestablishing intimacy, FANOS is a helpful tool to apply. If you struggle with identifying your emotions, you can also refer to the wheel of emotions when completing FANOS with your spouse/partner.

EXERCISE 5-2: FANOS CHECK-IN

In the following exercise, you will apply the concepts of FANOS in your relationship. The key to doing this exercise is being emotionally present, making eye contact, and not getting defensive. Discuss an appropriate time to complete this exercise in a face-to-face setting with your partner/spouse. Then jointly decide/commit to completing the exercise over the course of 30-60 minutes at a designated time without outside distractions. During the exercise, you can either take turns answering each prompt/question, or you can allow each other to cycle all the way through the entire exercise. Don't rush. Take your time focusing on each other and being empathically receptive to what is being said. Avoid the desire to engage in the drama triangle when emotions are triggered. The purpose of this exercise is to be vulnerable about where each of you are in your recovery. After the exercise is over, complete the reflection section to process with your individual therapist.

Debra Laaser – **FANOS**

FEELINGS – Share with your partner how you are feeling.

AFFIRMATION – How can I uplift my partner with praise?

NEEDS – What do I need in the relationship (emotionally, etc.)?

OWNERSHIP – What can I take ownership of in the relationship?

SOBRIETY/STRUGGLES – How is my sobriety going?

EXERCISE 5-3: REFLECTION ON FANOS CHECK-IN

Take a moment to reflect on the thoughts and emotions that were present during the FANOS check-in with your spouse/partner. Answer the following questions and process the exercise with your therapist/group.

1. What emotions come up when talking with your partner about your feelings and needs? How did you express those feelings/needs to your partner? _____

_____

_____

_____

2. How did your partner respond to your affirmations? What thoughts surfaced when reflecting on things you appreciate about your partner? _____

_____

_____

_____

3. What emotions/thoughts surfaced when taking ownership of issues in the relationship and your recovery? _____

_____

_____

_____

4. On a scale of 1-10, with 10 being high anxiety and 1 being low anxiety, where did you rate your anxiety pre-FANOS and post-FANOS with your partner? What are your thoughts concerning those numbers?_____

_____

_____

_____

5. How often can you commit to doing FANOS with your partner moving forward during the next 6 months? _____

_____

Now that we are beginning to reduce drama triangle transactions with our spouse/partner and communicate in healthy ways concerning how his or her acting-out/acting-in behavior has impacted the relationship, let's discuss the role of empathy in the healing process.

Empathy. Merriam-Webster's Dictionary defines empathy as, *"the action of understanding, being aware of, being sensitive to, and vicariously experiencing the feelings, thoughts, and experience of another of either the past or present without having the feelings, thoughts, and experience fully communicated in an objectively explicit manner."* Acting-out/acting-in desensitizes an individual to the pain he or she causes in the life of his or her spouse/partner/family. Developing empathy for those important individuals in your life is a skill that is imperative to recovery. This is evident via the 12-step model as the 9th step of making amends is based on this principle. Early in the recovery process, many individuals who have struggled with acting-out/acting-in are defensive toward their partner when their partner experiences triggers associated with his or her acting-out/acting-in behavior. Defensiveness/Anger posturing delays the recovery process by making the addict an emotionally unsafe person. If an addict is attempting to regain the trust of his or her partner post-disclosure, one can see how defensiveness/anger during a partner SA/IA triggering experience is traumatic. Remember, trajectories in relationship recovery are different for the addict versus the partner. An addict feels better after getting the addiction secret out. A partner's perception/trust in the addict is often shattered after disclosure, and he or she must work to heal the PTSD-like criteria that we address in the beginning of your recovery journey. The more you and your partner work to empathetically HEAR and FEEL each other's pain, the easier it is to rebuild trust in the relationship. A starting point for developing empathy can be the use of the therapeutic communication techniques called active listening and healthy assertiveness.

Active Listening and Healthy Assertiveness

Active Listening – The process of intently listening to your partner (i.e. not thinking of ways to counter your partner's assertions) while making eye contact with compassion. During this process, you are mirroring your body language to create a safe emotional space for your partner to express themselves (i.e. not scowling, sighing, rolling your eyes, or taking on a defensive posture, etc.). Once your partner finishes speaking/expressing themselves, paraphrase your partner's emotions and concerns to clarify if you heard them correctly.

Healthy Assertiveness – The process of using "I feel" statements to assert your feelings/beliefs/thoughts in an adult-to-adult manner (i.e. not a parent-to-child or child-to-child transaction in TA).

Example of using healthy assertiveness in an adult-to-adult manner: "I feel frustrated when I attempt to tell you about my day, and you seem disinterested by scrolling through your phone."

An example of a parent-to-child unhealthy use of assertiveness would be: "You need to look at me when I am talking to you when I get home from work."

An example of a child-to-child unhealthy use of assertiveness would be: "You are selfish person because you would rather sit there on your stupid phone than pay any attention to me. I hate you."

Using Active Listening and Healthy Assertiveness to articulate your hurt associated with your partner's acting out/acting in behavior and developing empathy for your partner's emotions despite your hurt.

Now that we have defined what active listening and healthy assertiveness are, let's explore how to adapt these concepts for using healthy assertiveness to articulate your emotions in healthy ways and developing empathy for your partner's emotions.

Example scenario: *You are out with your partner in public and an attractive individual walks by. You feel anxiety/anger when seeing your partner anxiously look away from that individual's direction.*

Partner: "I wasn't looking at them. I'm serious!"

You: "I'm feeling anxious and upset right now because doing something as simple as going out to dinner can be a trigger for our recovery. I hear you saying you are frustrated and weren't looking, but I want you to understand that this situation is very hurtful to me because my trust is damaged because you have been looking at other people in the past. There is also a part of me that is anxious and thinks that you subconsciously look at other females or males without realizing it is happening. When can we talk about this?

This is an example of using active listening and healthy assertiveness in a healthy way. Notice that the conversation was about your feelings, your partner's feelings, and wasn't focused primarily on fighting about who was "right" in the situation. It was an opportunity for your partner to know how his or her present and past behavior hurts you.

Now let's look at what an unempathetic response would look like:

Partner: "I wasn't looking at them. I'm serious!"

You: "Yeah sure you weren't. I saw you and I know what you are doing. Sometimes I really regret being in a relationship with you."

While your anger in the situation is valid, expressing it in a child-to-child or parent-to-child dynamic can damage the ability to build healing attachment in your relationship and potentially create triggering shame in your partner. Keep in mind that situations like the example on the previous page may trigger a PTSD-type trigger that makes you hypersensitive to your environment and it may be a challenge to respond in an adult-to-adult manner. This is normal but requires taking a moment to regulate your anxiety/anger before responding in emotion-mind.

EXERCISE 5-4: REFLECTION ON HEALTHY ASSERTIVENESS AND ACTIVE LISTENING

Now you know the difference between healthy and unhealthy ways to communicate your triggers and emotional hurt, list some self-regulations strategies you can use to get into wise mind before communicating your hurt to your partner the next time you experience a trauma trigger.

Strategy 1: _____

Strategy 2: _____

Strategy 3: _____

Strategy 4: _____

Strategy 5: _____

Strategy 6: _____

Week 20

DATE	EXERCISES TO COMPLETE
	Read pages 305-312 and complete exercises: 5-5 and 5-6

OBJECTIVES

- Learn the mechanics of the addiction cycle.
- Group processing of questions and insights regarding the psychoeducational aspects of the addiction cycle.

NOTES – INSIGHTS – THINGS TO EXPLORE IN THERAPY

_____
_____
_____
_____
_____
_____
_____
_____
_____

ACCOUNTABILITY ISSUES – GOALS FOR THE WEEK

_____
_____
_____
_____
_____
_____
_____
_____
_____
_____

PARTNER RECOVERY GROWTH INDEX (PRGI)

DENIAL 1 2 3 4 5 6 7 8 9 10

1 = Believing my partner isn't an addict, denying my partner's progress, and/or denying the hurt and pain I am feeling because of my partner's addiction.

10 = Consistently feeling/expressing the pain caused by my partner's behavior and adjusting boundaries when appropriate due to therapeutic insight and progress.

ANXIETY MANAGEMENT 1 2 3 4 5 6 7 8 9 10

1 = Avoiding anxiety triggers and anxious feelings/sensations in my body

10 = Acknowledging anxiety and using it to provide insight into what is important

ANGER MANAGEMENT 1 2 3 4 5 6 7 8 9 10

1 = Having explosive outbursts, making threats, yelling, stuffing, devaluing, withholding, and other child-like dynamics when experiencing anger

10 = Consistently expressing anger in an adult-to-adult dynamic and externally processing anger via the use of therapeutic tools

DEPRESSION MANAGEMENT 1 2 3 4 5 6 7 8 9 10

1 = Choosing to engage in the victim orientation via avoiding emotional processing, not practicing self-care, and self-loathing every day for the past 7+ days

10 = Consistently choosing to use therapeutic tools, practice self-care, and take behavioral baby steps towards one's mission statement in life every day for the past 14 days

SHAME MANAGEMENT 1 2 3 4 5 6 7 8 9 10

1 = Believing I'm a bad person or a mistake (i.e. I'm a bad wife/I'm unlovable)

10 = Believing I'm a good person who made some mistakes

CO-DEPENDENCY 1 2 3 4 5 6 7 8 9 10

1 = Exhibiting rescuing behavior, failure to set boundaries, failure to implement consequences for boundary failures, and failing to process one's own issues during the past 7+ days.

10 = I have set/executed boundaries, taken behavioral baby steps towards my individual mission statement, acknowledged/processed my emotions, and living a life that is more internally than externally motivated

BOUNDARIES | 1 2 3 4 5 6 7 8 9 10

1 = A total lack of boundaries or the use of vague boundaries to justify withholding.

10 = Consistently maintaining boundaries and implementing consequences when boundaries are violated.

TRUST | 1 2 3 4 5 6 7 8 9 10

1 = Obsessing about your partner's recovery (OCD/co-dependency/anxiety), ignoring your partner's recovery work (denial/avoidance) and/or doubting your ability to make good decisions in the past 7+ days

10 = Consistently allowing your boundaries/consequences to work for you, expressing emotions in healthy transparent ways during FANOS check-ins and working towards building healthy attachment.

ACTING-IN | 1 2 3 4 5 6 7 8 9 10

1 = I withheld emotional/spiritual/physical intimacy in the past 7 days

10 = 6+ months of continuous emotional/spiritual/physical engagement

FORGIVENESS | 1 2 3 4 5 6 7 8 9 10

1 = Holding onto anger/resentment/bitterness and refusing to consider forgiveness

10 = I have fully processed my grief, accepted the betrayal, set boundaries, and reached a level of peace due to forgiveness

CONFLICT RESOLUTION | 1 2 3 4 5 6 7 8 9 10

1 = Displaying parent-to-child or child-to-child dynamics during conflict or avoiding conflict via people pleasing behaviors

10 = Consistently using healthy assertiveness and active listening with empathy to resolve conflict or reach a compromise in life every day for the past 14 days

SELF-WORTH | 1 2 3 4 5 6 7 8 9 10

1 = Feeling/believing I'm inadequate every day in the past 7+ days

10 = Feeling/believing I'm an adequate individual whose worth is not tied to another individual's behavior each day for the past 3+ months

SELF-CARE | 1 2 3 4 5 6 7 8 9 10

1 = Neglecting self-care behaviors/No self-care behaviors during the past 7+ days

10 = Consistently practicing self-care behaviors each day for the past year

The addiction cycle taught in our program incorporates the work/models of Dr. Robert Weiss, Dr. Douglass Weiss, and Dr. Patrick Carnes. The model includes the concepts of Triggers (Pain Agents/Preoccupation), Fantasizing (Preoccupation), Ritualization, Acting-out/Acting-in (Compulsive behavior(s)/Compulsive withholding behaviors), Numbing, and Despair/Shame.

Addiction Cycle

The SA and IA Addiction Cycle

- Triggers *(Pain Agents)*
- Fantasizing
- Ritualization
- Acting-out / Acting-in
- Numbing
- Despair / Shame

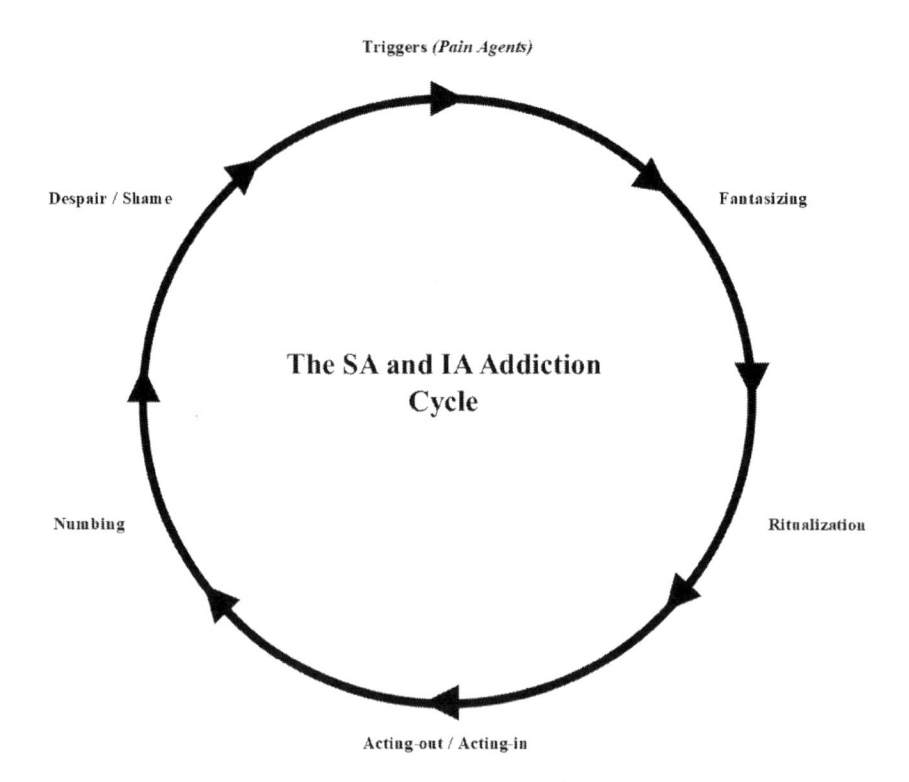

Dr. Douglas Weiss <u>4 Pain Agents</u>

1. Emotional Discomfort
2. Unresolved Conflict
3. Stress
4. A Need to Connect

The 4 pain agents are internal and external factors that drive acting out behavior. We view the pain agents as a part of the triggers/preoccupation stage of the acting out cycle. An important component of an addict's recovery is understanding and coping with his or her individual pain agents. How well your partner is managing his or her pain agents can be a behavioral indication as to if he or she is doing well in his or her recovery. Remember, it is not your job to micromanage your partner's recovery work, as this would be unhealthy rescuing behavior (co-dependency). If you see your partner not working his or her recovery in a healthy, productive manner, it is your responsibility to articulate your emotions about the situation and refer to your boundaries/consequences established in chapter 3 of this book.

EXERCISE 5-5: QUESTIONS ABOUT THE ADDICTION CYCLE

This exercise gives you the opportunity to have your questions answered about the addiction cycle in a group setting. List your questions below.

Question 1: _____

Question 2: _____

Question 3: _____

Question 4: _____

Notes/Answers:

_____

_____

_____

_____

_____

_____

_____

EXERCISE 5-6: REFLECTION QUESTIONS ABOUT THE ADDICTION CYCLE

This exercise is an opportunity to process your insights into your beliefs/emotions about the addiction cycle after the addiction cycle group processing psychoeducational exercise. List your responses to each question below.

1. What were your previous beliefs about addiction prior to the psychoeducational group processing exercise?

_____

_____

_____

2. What are your beliefs about addiction after the psychoeducational group processing exercise?

_____

_____

_____

3. What emotions surface when realizing that your partners addiction has created an internal shame and despair in his or her life?

___

___

___

4. Looking back on your relationship with your partner, what patterns do you notice about your partner's addiction cycle?

___

___

___

5. How do you apply what you have learned from this exercise moving forward?

___

___

___

Week 21

DATE	EXERCISES TO COMPLETE
	Read pages 313-323 and complete exercise: 6-1

OBJECTIVES

- Exploring where you are in the recovery process.
- Group processing of individual issues to be addressed as you continue your recovery journey.

NOTES – INSIGHTS – THINGS TO EXPLORE IN THERAPY

_____
_____
_____
_____
_____
_____
_____
_____
_____
_____

ACCOUNTABILITY ISSUES – GOALS FOR THE WEEK

_____
_____
_____
_____
_____
_____
_____
_____
_____
_____

PARTNER RECOVERY GROWTH INDEX (PRGI)

DENIAL | 1 2 3 4 5 6 7 8 9 10

1 = Believing my partner isn't an addict, denying my partner's progress, and/or denying the hurt and pain I am feeling because of my partner's addiction.

10 = Consistently feeling/expressing the pain caused by my partner's behavior and adjusting boundaries when appropriate due to therapeutic insight and progress.

ANXIETY MANAGEMENT | 1 2 3 4 5 6 7 8 9 10

1 = Avoiding anxiety triggers and anxious feelings/sensations in my body

10 = Acknowledging anxiety and using it to provide insight into what is important

ANGER MANAGEMENT | 1 2 3 4 5 6 7 8 9 10

1 = Having explosive outbursts, making threats, yelling, stuffing, devaluing, withholding, and other child-like dynamics when experiencing anger

10 = Consistently expressing anger in an adult-to-adult dynamic and externally processing anger via the use of therapeutic tools

DEPRESSION MANAGEMENT | 1 2 3 4 5 6 7 8 9 10

1 = Choosing to engage in the victim orientation via avoiding emotional processing, not practicing self-care, and self-loathing every day for the past 7+ days

10 = Consistently choosing to use therapeutic tools, practice self-care, and take behavioral baby steps towards one's mission statement in life every day for the past 14 days

SHAME MANAGEMENT | 1 2 3 4 5 6 7 8 9 10

1 = Believing I'm a bad person or a mistake (i.e. I'm a bad wife/I'm unlovable)

10 = Believing I'm a good person who made some mistakes

CO-DEPENDENCY | 1 2 3 4 5 6 7 8 9 10

1 = Exhibiting rescuing behavior, failure to set boundaries, failure to implement consequences for boundary failures, and failing to process one's own issues during the past 7+ days.

10 = I have set/executed boundaries, taken behavioral baby steps towards my individual mission statement, acknowledged/processed my emotions, and living a life that is more internally than externally motivated

BOUNDARIES | 1 2 3 4 5 6 7 8 9 10

1 = A total lack of boundaries or the use of vague boundaries to justify withholding.

10 = Consistently maintaining boundaries and implementing consequences when boundaries are violated.

TRUST | 1 2 3 4 5 6 7 8 9 10

1 = Obsessing about your partner's recovery (OCD/co-dependency/anxiety), ignoring your partner's recovery work (denial/avoidance) and/or doubting your ability to make good decisions in the past 7+ days

10 = Consistently allowing your boundaries/consequences to work for you, expressing emotions in healthy transparent ways during FANOS check-ins and working towards building healthy attachment.

ACTING-IN | 1 2 3 4 5 6 7 8 9 10

1 = I withheld emotional/spiritual/physical intimacy in the past 7 days

10 = 6+ months of continuous emotional/spiritual/physical engagement

FORGIVENESS | 1 2 3 4 5 6 7 8 9 10

1 = Holding onto anger/resentment/bitterness and refusing to consider forgiveness

10 = I have fully processed my grief, accepted the betrayal, set boundaries, and reached a level of peace due to forgiveness

CONFLICT RESOLUTION | 1 2 3 4 5 6 7 8 9 10

1 = Displaying parent-to-child or child-to-child dynamics during conflict or avoiding conflict via people pleasing behaviors

10 = Consistently using healthy assertiveness and active listening with empathy to resolve conflict or reach a compromise in life every day for the past 14 days

SELF-WORTH | 1 2 3 4 5 6 7 8 9 10

1 = Feeling/believing I'm inadequate every day in the past 7+ days

10 = Feeling/believing I'm an adequate individual whose worth is not tied to another individual's behavior each day for the past 3+ months

SELF-CARE | 1 2 3 4 5 6 7 8 9 10

1 = Neglecting self-care behaviors/No self-care behaviors during the past 7+ days

10 = Consistently practicing self-care behaviors each day for the past year

Chapter 6: Developing a Vision and Moving Forward

At this point in your recovery journey, you are likely starting to gain a new perspective on the following: your life, your partner and his or her acting out/acting in behavior, and how you truly feel about the betrayal(s) you have experienced. Hopefully, you have concluded that your partner's acting out/acting in behavior was not because you are not good enough, but it is a product of his or her decision to cope with the pain agents of life in unhealthy ways. For some of you, this realization has altered your perception of yourself and created a sense of empowerment in your life and relationship. This group of individuals has likely stuck to their boundaries and consequences and their partners have either worked their recovery or faced the reality of losing their relationships due to his or her choice to not get well. Another portion of you is still in the middle of the grieving process and unsure if you can get past the betrayal and trust again. Maybe your partner is working on his or her recovery or maybe they are still slipping and breaking sobriety. If this is you, stay strong and continue to work on your recovery while sticking to your boundaries and consequences. The last group of you may feel that not much has changed with you or your partner. If you fall into this group, now is the time to take inventory of where you are at, why you are here, and what you can behaviorally do about it to move forward. All the groups mentioned in this text can benefit from the work in this chapter. Whether you feel you are trending in the right direction or not, everyone can benefit from developing a healthy vision and taking realistic behavioral action steps to progress towards the vision. Steven Covey, author of the 7 habits, states that it is important to "begin with the end in mind." Thus, before developing a plan of action, we must reflect on what we want to pursue and why it is important to us. At this point, you understand that the drama and chaos of addictive systems can separate you from yourself and your authentic identity. For the co-dependent partner, managing your partner's addiction HAS been your identity. It can feel emotionally overwhelming to realize that perhaps your own addiction, acting-in, or insecurities have led you to seek relationships with people looking for rescuers. Now is the time to change that course, but we don't want to swing so far towards the other side of the pendulum that we become self-absorbed and unempathetic towards others. Healthy visions are rooted in balance, mindfulness, healthy spirituality, and daring to live an authentic life that doesn't feature masking or boundaryless compliance. It is okay to be who God made you to be. Despite what you have felt or experienced in your life, God has a plan and a purpose for you. In the book, *Finding Faith: 10 Things I Learned During Tribulation*, I recall a moment in life many years ago when I was ready to give up. Separated from my wife and walking through the aftermath of my mother's diagnosis with brain cancer, I found myself driving down back country roads in rural South Carolina, contemplating if I was ready to end it all. I punched the gas, raced down a long straight away, contemplating which light pole to hit. Before I had a moment to jerk the wheel, I received a text message from a friend, who later became my wife, telling me that they needed me in their life. It was a God moment. I slammed on the brakes and tearfully laughed. I thanked God for showing up and realized how far I had fallen into the drama triangle. It was time to disengage the drama triangle, stop playing the victim, and develop a healthy vision for life. The funny thing is, if you had told me at that time that the difficult experiences of my life would be the catalyst for change in the lives of others, I would have told you that you were crazy. Yet, God had other plans. Maybe what you are going through is similar. Maybe there have been times in your life or recovery journey that you wanted to give up. Maybe there were times you have felt like a victim and needed a rescuer and have been waiting on that rescuer to show up. The reality is, God equips us, but requires us to do the work to rescue ourselves. This shift in perspective can be anxiety-inducing, but it is important to remember that you are not alone. Over the past few months of your group work, you have built a healthy support system to help hold you accountable to the vision work you will do in this chapter. The time has come to move forward, but first, we must take inventory of where we have been and tell our story to the person who has hurt us the most. Let's get to work!

EXERCISE 6-1: TAKING INVENTORY (Part A)

In this cumulative exercise, you will go back and review some of the previous exercises to take an inventory of where you are in the recovery process. Enter your thoughts/takeaways from each exercise in the corresponding sections below.

1. Review exercise 1-3 (Healthy Expectations Worksheet). On a scale of 1-10, with 10 being 100% meeting expectations and 1 being less than 10% of meeting expectations, where do you currently rate your recovery? Explain your rationale. If your number is low, take a moment to review the Recovery Roadblocks list in chapter one and list any roadblocks that are limiting your success.

_____

_____

_____

_____

_____

_____

_____

EXERCISE 6-1: TAKING INVENTORY (Part A)

2. Review your weekly PRGI inventories for the entire group. What areas have seen the most growth and in what areas do you get to do some more therapeutic work? Explain your rationale.

_____

_____

_____

_____

_____

_____

3. Review exercise 2-1 (Developing a Self-Care Plan). What areas are you doing well practicing self-care and in what areas do you get to improve?

_____

_____

_____

_____

_____

_____

EXERCISE 6-1: TAKING INVENTORY (Part A)

4. Review exercise 5-1 (What Is My Role In The Drama). What areas are you doing well disengaging the drama triangle and in what areas do you get to improve? Explain your rationale.

EXERCISE 6-1: TAKING INVENTORY (Part B)

Take a moment to reflect on your responses to the first 4 questions from Part A of this exercise. Consolidate the information into a list of the top 5 issues to address in your individual recovery.

Issue #1:_____

Issue #2:_____

Issue #3:_____

Issue #4:_____

Issue #5:_____

Issue #6:_____

Week 22

DATE	EXERCISES TO COMPLETE
	Read pages 324-333 and complete exercises: 6-2 and 6-3

OBJECTIVES

- Exploring the importance of telling your story.
- Group processing of your impact letter.

NOTES – INSIGHTS – THINGS TO EXPLORE IN THERAPY

ACCOUNTABILITY ISSUES – GOALS FOR THE WEEK

PARTNER RECOVERY GROWTH INDEX (PRGI)

DENIAL 1 2 3 4 5 6 7 8 9 10

1 = Believing my partner isn't an addict, denying my partner's progress, and/or denying the hurt and pain I am feeling because of my partner's addiction.

10 = Consistently feeling/expressing the pain caused by my partner's behavior and adjusting boundaries when appropriate due to therapeutic insight and progress.

ANXIETY MANAGEMENT 1 2 3 4 5 6 7 8 9 10

1 = Avoiding anxiety triggers and anxious feelings/sensations in my body

10 = Acknowledging anxiety and using it to provide insight into what is important

ANGER MANAGEMENT 1 2 3 4 5 6 7 8 9 10

1 = Having explosive outbursts, making threats, yelling, stuffing, devaluing, withholding, and other child-like dynamics when experiencing anger

10 = Consistently expressing anger in an adult-to-adult dynamic and externally processing anger via the use of therapeutic tools

DEPRESSION MANAGEMENT 1 2 3 4 5 6 7 8 9 10

1 = Choosing to engage in the victim orientation via avoiding emotional processing, not practicing self-care, and self-loathing every day for the past 7+ days

10 = Consistently choosing to use therapeutic tools, practice self-care, and take behavioral baby steps towards one's mission statement in life every day for the past 14 days

SHAME MANAGEMENT 1 2 3 4 5 6 7 8 9 10

1 = Believing I'm a bad person or a mistake (i.e. I'm a bad wife/I'm unlovable)

10 = Believing I'm a good person who made some mistakes

CO-DEPENDENCY 1 2 3 4 5 6 7 8 9 10

1 = Exhibiting rescuing behavior, failure to set boundaries, failure to implement consequences for boundary failures, and failing to process one's own issues during the past 7+ days.

10 = I have set/executed boundaries, taken behavioral baby steps towards my individual mission statement, acknowledged/processed my emotions, and living a life that is more internally than externally motivated

BOUNDARIES | 1 2 3 4 5 6 7 8 9 10

1 = A total lack of boundaries or the use of vague boundaries to justify withholding.

10 = Consistently maintaining boundaries and implementing consequences when boundaries are violated.

TRUST | 1 2 3 4 5 6 7 8 9 10

1 = Obsessing about your partner's recovery (OCD/co-dependency/anxiety), ignoring your partner's recovery work (denial/avoidance) and/or doubting your ability to make good decisions in the past 7+ days

10 = Consistently allowing your boundaries/consequences to work for you, expressing emotions in healthy transparent ways during FANOS check-ins and working towards building healthy attachment.

ACTING-IN | 1 2 3 4 5 6 7 8 9 10

1 = I withheld emotional/spiritual/physical intimacy in the past 7 days

10 = 6+ months of continuous emotional/spiritual/physical engagement

FORGIVENESS | 1 2 3 4 5 6 7 8 9 10

1 = Holding onto anger/resentment/bitterness and refusing to consider forgiveness

10 = I have fully processed my grief, accepted the betrayal, set boundaries, and reached a level of peace due to forgiveness

CONFLICT RESOLUTION | 1 2 3 4 5 6 7 8 9 10

1 = Displaying parent-to-child or child-to-child dynamics during conflict or avoiding conflict via people pleasing behaviors

10 = Consistently using healthy assertiveness and active listening with empathy to resolve conflict or reach a compromise in life every day for the past 14 days

SELF-WORTH | 1 2 3 4 5 6 7 8 9 10

1 = Feeling/believing I'm inadequate every day in the past 7+ days

10 = Feeling/believing I'm an adequate individual whose worth is not tied to another individual's behavior each day for the past 3+ months

SELF-CARE | 1 2 3 4 5 6 7 8 9 10

1 = Neglecting self-care behaviors/No self-care behaviors during the past 7+ days

10 = Consistently practicing self-care behaviors each day for the past year

EXERCISE 6-2: TELLING YOUR STORY – IMPACT LETTER

Review exercises 4-1 (Impact Inventory), 4-9 (Inventory of Losses), and 4-10 (Reflection on Inventory of Losses). Use the space provided to write an impact letter to your partner about how his or her acting out/acting in behavior has impacted your life. Take your time on this exercise and allow yourself to flip back and forth to remind yourself of the facts associated with your partner's behavior. Make sure your letter is written in wise-mind and not driven by emotion-minded rage or resentment. You want to make sure that your story is heard and not discounted due to the language you are using. Process this letter with your therapist before sharing the letter with your partner. **You may want to process the letter with your partner in a joint session if you need support, and he or she may need to schedule a follow-up session with his or her therapist to process their emotions associated with your letter.** If you are no longer in a relationship with your partner, you do not want to share the letter with them and can process the letter with your therapist via an empty chair technique. Remember that this is your story, your feelings are valid, and you get to be honest about your experiences.

EXERCISE 6-2: TELLING YOUR STORY – IMPACT LETTER

Dear _____,

EXERCISE 6-2: TELLING YOUR STORY – IMPACT LETTER

EXERCISE 6-2: TELLING YOUR STORY – IMPACT LETTER

EXERCISE 6-2: TELLING YOUR STORY – IMPACT LETTER

_____

_____

_____

_____

_____

_____

_____

_____

_____

_____

_____

_____

Sincerely,

_____

EXERCISE 6-3: REFLECTION ON SHARING YOUR IMPACT LETTER

1. What emotions surfaced when sharing your impact letter with your partner and/or your therapist/life coach?

_____

_____

_____

2. Now that you have shared your story as a partner of someone who struggles with sexual acting out and/or intimacy anorexia, what thoughts do you have about yourself in relation to your experiences?

_____

_____

_____

_____

_____

_____

_____

_____

3. What have you learned about yourself during your own individual journey of recovery?

_____

_____

_____

_____

_____

_____

_____

4. What lessons about yourself and your relationships with others can you apply as you move forward in life?

_____

_____

_____

_____

_____

_____

_____

_____

Week 23

DATE	EXERCISES TO COMPLETE
	Read pages 334-347 and complete exercise: 6-4

OBJECTIVES

- Exploring the importance of developing a healthy vision post-betrayal.
- Group processing of your vision board.

NOTES – INSIGHTS – THINGS TO EXPLORE IN THERAPY

ACCOUNTABILITY ISSUES – GOALS FOR THE WEEK

PARTNER RECOVERY GROWTH INDEX (PRGI)

DENIAL 1 2 3 4 5 6 7 8 9 10

1 = Believing my partner isn't an addict, denying my partner's progress, and/or denying the hurt and pain I am feeling because of my partner's addiction.

10 = Consistently feeling/expressing the pain caused by my partner's behavior and adjusting boundaries when appropriate due to therapeutic insight and progress.

ANXIETY MANAGEMENT 1 2 3 4 5 6 7 8 9 10

1 = Avoiding anxiety triggers and anxious feelings/sensations in my body

10 = Acknowledging anxiety and using it to provide insight into what is important

ANGER MANAGEMENT 1 2 3 4 5 6 7 8 9 10

1 = Having explosive outbursts, making threats, yelling, stuffing, devaluing, withholding, and other child-like dynamics when experiencing anger

10 = Consistently expressing anger in an adult-to-adult dynamic and externally processing anger via the use of therapeutic tools

DEPRESSION MANAGEMENT 1 2 3 4 5 6 7 8 9 10

1 = Choosing to engage in the victim orientation via avoiding emotional processing, not practicing self-care, and self-loathing every day for the past 7+ days

10 = Consistently choosing to use therapeutic tools, practice self-care, and take behavioral baby steps towards one's mission statement in life every day for the past 14 days

SHAME MANAGEMENT 1 2 3 4 5 6 7 8 9 10

1 = Believing I'm a bad person or a mistake (i.e. I'm a bad wife/I'm unlovable)

10 = Believing I'm a good person who made some mistakes

CO-DEPENDENCY 1 2 3 4 5 6 7 8 9 10

1 = Exhibiting rescuing behavior, failure to set boundaries, failure to implement consequences for boundary failures, and failing to process one's own issues during the past 7+ days.

10 = I have set/executed boundaries, taken behavioral baby steps towards my individual mission statement, acknowledged/processed my emotions, and living a life that is more internally than externally motivated

BOUNDARIES 1 2 3 4 5 6 7 8 9 10

1 = A total lack of boundaries or the use of vague boundaries to justify withholding.

10 = Consistently maintaining boundaries and implementing consequences when boundaries are violated.

TRUST 1 2 3 4 5 6 7 8 9 10

1 = Obsessing about your partner's recovery (OCD/co-dependency/anxiety), ignoring your partner's recovery work (denial/avoidance) and/or doubting your ability to make good decisions in the past 7+ days

10 = Consistently allowing your boundaries/consequences to work for you, expressing emotions in healthy transparent ways during FANOS check-ins and working towards building healthy attachment.

ACTING-IN 1 2 3 4 5 6 7 8 9 10

1 = I withheld emotional/spiritual/physical intimacy in the past 7 days

10 = 6+ months of continuous emotional/spiritual/physical engagement

FORGIVENESS 1 2 3 4 5 6 7 8 9 10

1 = Holding onto anger/resentment/bitterness and refusing to consider forgiveness

10 = I have fully processed my grief, accepted the betrayal, set boundaries, and reached a level of peace due to forgiveness

CONFLICT RESOLUTION 1 2 3 4 5 6 7 8 9 10

1 = Displaying parent-to-child or child-to-child dynamics during conflict or avoiding conflict via people pleasing behaviors

10 = Consistently using healthy assertiveness and active listening with empathy to resolve conflict or reach a compromise in life every day for the past 14 days

SELF-WORTH 1 2 3 4 5 6 7 8 9 10

1 = Feeling/believing I'm inadequate every day in the past 7+ days

10 = Feeling/believing I'm an adequate individual whose worth is not tied to another individual's behavior each day for the past 3+ months

SELF-CARE 1 2 3 4 5 6 7 8 9 10

1 = Neglecting self-care behaviors/No self-care behaviors during the past 7+ days

10 = Consistently practicing self-care behaviors each day for the past year

Developing a Vision is the ability to cognitively reflect on the here and now with insight while developing a plan for one's future. The past few months, or perhaps years, have been a process of confronting trauma, pain, anxiety, shame, grief, and aspects of reality that are difficult to accept. Wherever you are on this journey, you can make a wise-minded choice of behaviorally pursuing a healthy vision today. People who get stuck in the drama triangle of addictive and co-dependent systems focus on the problem-centric nature of their experiences. They focus on the losses, pain, unmet expectations, and discontent that drive emotion-minded decision-making which perpetuates the addictive and co-dependent systems. Resilient people acknowledge the pain and losses of the past but choose to progress forward via a realistic vision for their lives. They refuse to focus on what they cannot change and choose to change the things they can. If this statement sounds familiar, you are likely aware of Reinhold Niebuhr's serenity prayer which reads:

> *God, grant me the serenity to accept the things I cannot change, the courage to change the things I can, and the wisdom to know the difference. Living one day at a time; accepting hardship as a pathway to peace; taking, as Jesus*

> *did, this sinful world as it is, not as I would have it; trusting that You will make all things right if I surrender to Your will; so that I may be reasonably happy in this life and supremely happy with You forever in the next. Amen.*

The serenity prayer embodies a healthy balance between an external and internal locus of control. People who are overly reliant on an external locus of control attempt to set goals based on the praise and validation of others. People who are overly reliant on an internal locus of control discount the healthy feedback of others. A healthy vision is rooted in what is important to you (internal locus of control) but practical (external locus of control). For example, a healthy vision for someone who experienced marital betrayal would not rest entirely on his or her addicted partner's behavior (external locus of control). On the other side of the spectrum, the individual in this situation overly reliant on an internal locus of control would allow their emotion-mind or reason-mind to dictate his or her vision void of the external consequences. Both visions would ultimately lack the wise-mind balance necessary for a healthy future. The healthy vision for someone who has experienced relational betrayal would rest on his or her belief system, healthy needs/expectations, and accountability for those around them to respect those beliefs and needs (balanced internal and external locus of control). Sometimes an external locus of control is driven by childhood trauma. In **EXERCISE 2-5: CONNECTING TO YOUR INNER CHILD**, we explored various cognitive beliefs associated with painful experiences. As you begin the process of developing your vision, be sure to reflect on the driving forces behind your belief system. Wise-minded visions are not driven by protector or controlling parts, parental expectations or the expectations of unhealthy people in life. They are driven by the inner-adult. It is imperative to work with your counselor and/or coach during the vision development and action step process as this journey can often use unbiased feedback from a professional support system who understand the complex dynamics of internal and external motivators. The following exercises are designed to facilitate the development of your new vision. Make sure you take the appropriate time to reflect on your responses and consult with your support team.

EXERCISE 6-4: CREATING A VISION BOARD (Part A)

A Vision Board is a tool for visualizing your future goals for life. Using graphics, pictures, drawings, and text, a vision board allows an individual to experience inspiration to take short-term behavioral action steps towards his or her vision until the outcome has been achieved. Before you begin this process, take a moment below to reflect on **EXERCISE 6-1: TAKING INVENTORY (Part B)** and **question 4** of **EXERCISE 6-3: REFLECTION ON SHARING YOUR IMPACT LETTER**. While you do not want your vision to be problem-centered, reviewing what you have learned about yourself during your therapeutic journey can provide insight into issues or barriers to address to make your vision attainable. Answer the following questions and discuss this exercise with your therapist/life coach before proceeding to part B.

1. What specific traits about myself make me unique?

_____

_____

_____

2. What values/beliefs/interests motivate me to pursue goals in life?

3. What activities/behaviors connect me with my true self?

4. What activities/behaviors comfortably connect me with others?

5. What activities/behaviors connect me with my Higher Power?

6. What activities/behaviors connect me with purpose in life?

_____

_____

_____

_____

_____

_____

_____

_____

7. What activities/behaviors reduce my progression towards purpose?

_____

_____

_____

_____

_____

_____

8. Close your eyes and visualize your future self in 1, 5, 10, and 20 years. What are you behaviorally doing? What is your vocation? What do your relationships look like? What is bringing you contentment?

EXERCISE 6-4: CREATING A VISION BOARD (Part B)

Now that you have reflected on what is important to you in life, it is time to create a vision board. In the space below, draw some images that represent your vision for the future. Remember, the vision board is not problem-centric and will focus on where you are going in life. Once you have a general idea of what you want, use a giant piece of posterboard, cardboard, or artistic paper to create your vision board with printed images, cut outs, text, etc. Share your vision board with your therapist/life coach, and group.

EXERCISE 6-4: CREATING A VISION BOARD (Part B)

EXERCISE 6-4: CREATING A VISION BOARD (Part B)

Week 24

DATE	EXERCISES TO COMPLETE
	Read pages 348-360 and complete exercises: 6-5, 6-6, and 6-7

OBJECTIVES

- Taking inventory of your PRGI from the past 24 weeks.
- Exploring your biggest takeaways from the group.
- Group processing of where you go from here.

NOTES – INSIGHTS – THINGS TO EXPLORE IN THERAPY

_____
_____
_____
_____
_____
_____
_____
_____
_____
_____

ACCOUNTABILITY ISSUES – GOALS FOR THE WEEK

_____
_____
_____
_____
_____
_____
_____
_____
_____
_____

PARTNER RECOVERY GROWTH INDEX (PRGI)

DENIAL | 1 2 3 4 5 6 7 8 9 10

1 = Believing my partner isn't an addict, denying my partner's progress, and/or denying the hurt and pain I am feeling because of my partner's addiction.

10 = Consistently feeling/expressing the pain caused by my partner's behavior and adjusting boundaries when appropriate due to therapeutic insight and progress.

ANXIETY MANAGEMENT | 1 2 3 4 5 6 7 8 9 10

1 = Avoiding anxiety triggers and anxious feelings/sensations in my body

10 = Acknowledging anxiety and using it to provide insight into what is important

ANGER MANAGEMENT | 1 2 3 4 5 6 7 8 9 10

1 = Having explosive outbursts, making threats, yelling, stuffing, devaluing, withholding, and other child-like dynamics when experiencing anger

10 = Consistently expressing anger in an adult-to-adult dynamic and externally processing anger via the use of therapeutic tools

DEPRESSION MANAGEMENT | 1 2 3 4 5 6 7 8 9 10

1 = Choosing to engage in the victim orientation via avoiding emotional processing, not practicing self-care, and self-loathing every day for the past 7+ days

10 = Consistently choosing to use therapeutic tools, practice self-care, and take behavioral baby steps towards one's mission statement in life every day for the past 14 days

SHAME MANAGEMENT | 1 2 3 4 5 6 7 8 9 10

1 = Believing I'm a bad person or a mistake (i.e. I'm a bad wife/I'm unlovable)

10 = Believing I'm a good person who made some mistakes

CO-DEPENDENCY | 1 2 3 4 5 6 7 8 9 10

1 = Exhibiting rescuing behavior, failure to set boundaries, failure to implement consequences for boundary failures, and failing to process one's own issues during the past 7+ days.

10 = I have set/executed boundaries, taken behavioral baby steps towards my individual mission statement, acknowledged/processed my emotions, and living a life that is more internally than externally motivated

BOUNDARIES | 1 2 3 4 5 6 7 8 9 10

1 = A total lack of boundaries or the use of vague boundaries to justify withholding.

10 = Consistently maintaining boundaries and implementing consequences when boundaries are violated.

TRUST | 1 2 3 4 5 6 7 8 9 10

1 = Obsessing about your partner's recovery (OCD/co-dependency/anxiety), ignoring your partner's recovery work (denial/avoidance) and/or doubting your ability to make good decisions in the past 7+ days

10 = Consistently allowing your boundaries/consequences to work for you, expressing emotions in healthy transparent ways during FANOS check-ins and working towards building healthy attachment.

ACTING-IN | 1 2 3 4 5 6 7 8 9 10

1 = I withheld emotional/spiritual/physical intimacy in the past 7 days

10 = 6+ months of continuous emotional/spiritual/physical engagement

FORGIVENESS | 1 2 3 4 5 6 7 8 9 10

1 = Holding onto anger/resentment/bitterness and refusing to consider forgiveness

10 = I have fully processed my grief, accepted the betrayal, set boundaries, and reached a level of peace due to forgiveness

CONFLICT RESOLUTION | 1 2 3 4 5 6 7 8 9 10

1 = Displaying parent-to-child or child-to-child dynamics during conflict or avoiding conflict via people pleasing behaviors

10 = Consistently using healthy assertiveness and active listening with empathy to resolve conflict or reach a compromise in life every day for the past 14 days

SELF-WORTH | 1 2 3 4 5 6 7 8 9 10

1 = Feeling/believing I'm inadequate every day in the past 7+ days

10 = Feeling/believing I'm an adequate individual whose worth is not tied to another individual's behavior each day for the past 3+ months

SELF-CARE | 1 2 3 4 5 6 7 8 9 10

1 = Neglecting self-care behaviors/No self-care behaviors during the past 7+ days

10 = Consistently practicing self-care behaviors each day for the past year

EXERCISE 6-5: DIALOGUE WITH YOUR FUTURE SELF

In this final therapeutic exercise, you will write a letter to your future self in the latter days of your life. Imagine yourself with 95% of your life behind you, and in this letter, you are taking the time to reminisce on your journey of life to that very moment in time. Speak from the heart. Be honest. What is important? What empathetic words do you have for your future self? What regrets do you have? What legacy have you left? What have you learned? What have you accomplished? These are just a few questions to ponder as you reflect on the remaining years of your life and recovery journey.

Dear _____,

_____

_____

_____

_____

_____

_____

EXERCISE 6-5: DIALOGUE WITH YOUR FUTURE SELF

EXERCISE 6-5: DIALOGUE WITH YOUR FUTURE SELF

EXERCISE 6-5: DIALOGUE WITH YOUR FUTURE SELF

_____
_____
_____
_____
_____
_____
_____
_____
_____
_____

With love,

_____

EXERCISE 6-6: REFLECTIONS ON THE DIALOGUE WITH YOUR FUTURE SELF

Take a moment to reflect on your individual and group processing of your dialogue with your future self. List your responses to each question below.

1. What emotions surfaced when reading your letter to your future self?

_____

_____

_____

2. What surprised you about your perception of yourself in the letter?

_____

_____

_____

3. What do you get to change in your life today to help you progress towards your vision?

_____

_____

_____

4. What support do you need to make these changes?

_____

_____

_____

5. What was your biggest takeaway from the dialogue with self exercise?

_____

_____

_____

EXERCISE 6-7: PUTTING IT ALL TOGETHER: TAKING A 24 WEEK INVENTORY OF YOUR PARTNER RECOVERY GROWTH INDEX (PRGI)

In this exercise, you will Reflect on the past 24 weeks of entries from your Partner Recovery Growth Index (PRGI).

1. Compare your PRGI inventory from pages 33-45 to your inventories over the past 22 weeks. What differences do you see and what is your rationale for the scores you have today?

_____

_____

_____

_____

_____

_____

_____

_____

_____

_____

2. What were your biggest growth areas from the PRGI?

3. What were your biggest takeaways from your participation in the program?

Closing thoughts and new beginnings. We began this text by focusing on the complexity of recovery for addicts and their partners. At this point in the recovery process, the picture of where you get to go from here is likely coming into focus. For some of you, time, boundaries, and therapeutic work by you and your partner have led to the possibility of reconciliation. At this stage, it might be necessary to begin joint sessions. For others, you may have come to realize that reconciliation is not possible. Wherever you are in this process, remember that good decisions are made in wise mind. Any decision made in emotion mind or reason mind could lead to regret. So what are the next steps?

Now that you have created a visual representation of your vision, the next few weeks, months, and years will be about developing and executing action steps to progress towards the vision. Your therapist/life coach, support groups, accountability partners, and Higher Power are all a part of this developmental journey. While obstacles and roadblocks will likely arise on your journey, the individual in control of your future destination is you. Remember the lessons you have learned about yourself throughout this book. It is not easy to do the work you have done, so remember to show yourself grace when setbacks occur. Be patient with yourself and continue to work on your plan for self-care. Also, make sure you are taking some time for mindfulness via prayer or meditation. Life has meaning when we focus on being present in the moment and doing what matters. In relationships, hold those you love accountable via healthy boundaries and consequences. Use healthy assertiveness and active listening when communicating and do not allow anxiety to be the driving force in your behavior. In new relationships, do the same and be honest about where you are at in your recovery. Do not allow the fear of being alone to cause a boundary breakdown or emotion-minded compromise in your belief system. Once you have developed your action step plan with your therapist/life coach, each new day is an opportunity to take one step closer to your vision's destination. If you follow your path, one day you will be the change you are currently pursuing.

Notes:

References

The following books, articles, and websites influenced the writing of this book.

Carnes, Patrick. *Facing the Shadow: Starting Sexual and Relationship Recovery*. (3rd). Gentle Path Press. 2015.

Carnes, Patrick. *Recovery Zone Vol. 1: Making Lasting Change - The Internal Tasks*. Gentle Path Press, 2009.

Carnes, Patrick. *Recovery Zone Vol. 2: Achieving Balance in Your Life – The External Tasks*. Gentle Path Press, 2021.

Weiss, Douglas. *The Final Freedom*. Charisma House, 1998.

Weiss, Douglas. *Intimacy Anorexia: Healing the Hidden Addiction in Your Marriage*. Discovery Press, 2016.

Weiss, Robert. *Sex Addiction 101: A Basic Guide to Healing from Sex, Porn, and Love Addiction*. Health Communications Inc, 2015.

Emerald, David. *The Power of TED: The Empowerment Dynamic*. Polaris Publishing, 2016.

Laaser, Debra. *Shattered Vows: Hope and Healing for Women Who Have Been Sexually Betrayed*. Zondervan, 2008

Karpman, Stephen. *The Drama Triangle*. http://www.karpmandramatriangle.com, 2005-2015.

Linehan, Marsha. *Wise Mind Model*. https://.therapeuticoasis.com/living-in-wise-mind-dbt-skills-for-everyone, 2016.

Schwartz, Richard. *The Internal Family Systems Model Outline*. https://ifs-institute.com/resources/articles/internal-family-systems-model-outline, 1995-2025

Merriam Webster. https://www.merriam-webster.com, 2022.